AN INTRODUCTION TO
MODERN
POLITICAL THEORY

Owing to the antiquity and rarity of this book, certain pages are regrettably absent, and readability is compromised due to the blurring of the original text. If you possess any insights regarding the availability of these missing sections, kindly inform us. Your assistance is crucial in ensuring the completion of this significant work for the benefit of future generations.

AN INTRODUCTION TO MODERN POLITICAL THEORY

C. E. M. JOAD

GYAN

Published by

GYAN

Gyan Publishing House
5, Ansari Road
Daryaganj, New Delhi-110002
Phone: 011-47034999, 9811692060
E-mail: books@gyanbooks.com

Distribution Network
gyanbooks.com
India, USA, Canada, UK, Australia

ISBN: 978-93-6920-323-9 (HB)

First Published, 1924

2nd Impression 2025

Printed at: Gyan Press, Delhi.

AN INTRODUCTION TO MODERN POLITICAL THEORY
Author: C. E. M. JOAD

KARL MARX

Introduction to MODERN POLITICAL THEORY

BY

C. E. M. JOAD

OXFORD
AT THE CLARENDON PRESS
1924

CONTENTS

PAGE

Introduction 7

1. The Idealist Theory of the State 9
2. Modern Individualism 24
3. Socialism: with special reference to Collectivism . 39
4. Syndicalism and Guild Socialism 61
5. Communism and Anarchism 86
6. Problems of Socialist Theory 112

Bibliography 124

INTRODUCTION

I HAVE endeavoured in the succeeding pages to present in outline the most important aspects of modern political thought, my aim being throughout to describe and to discuss the various theories in such a way that no previous acquaintance with the subject shall be necessary for their comprehension.

Modern political theory is, however, in a state of considerable confusion; not only are the matters which it discusses of a highly controversial nature, but there is disagreement both as to the character of its central problems, and as to the appropriate methods of treating them. For this reason the task of describing the most important aspects of modern political thought is not an easy one. I am fully aware that many of the topics usually discussed in political theory find little or no place in the succeeding chapters. The Idealist theory of the State is allotted a bare dozen pages, and is treated mainly as a background to the various reactions it has provoked; Individualism is dismissed in an equally summary fashion, and consideration of the relationship between law and politics there is none. On the other hand I shall seem to some to have devoted a disproportionate amount of space to recent developments in Socialist theory. This apparent disparity of treatment is not intended to imply any disparagement of the merits of Idealist or Individualist theory as compared with those of Socialism; it simply reflects the tendencies prevalent in political theory to-day.

The great majority of the books on this subject which have appeared in recent years are devoted to a treatment of various aspects of Socialism, and most of them are written more or less definitely from a Socialist standpoint. Even those writers who are hostile to Socialism spend most of their time in criticizing it.

Thus Socialism cccupies the centre of interest even when it does not take pride of place, and the questions, with which writers chiefly concern themselves to-day, relate on the theoretical side to the conceptions of functional democracy and of the personality of the group, and on the practical side to the various forms of Socialist doctrine in which these conceptions find expression.

These developments, which are distinctively modern, are profoundly significant, not only in themselves, but also in their bearing upon the question of the powers and functions of the State. They affect State action in practice, and they are likely to affect it more in the future; so that, apart altogether from their philosophical interest, it becomes important for the writer of an introduction to modern political theory to describe them in some detail.

My thanks are due to Mr. G. D. H. Cole for kindly reading through Chapters 3, 4, and 5, and for making many valuable suggestions which have been adopted.

C. E. M. J.

I

The Idealist Theory of the State

Introductory.

THE Idealist or Absolutist theory of the State forms an integral part of the great tradition of philosophical Idealism which, until quite recent years, may be said to have been the dominating influence in English political thought. It is a theory which, assuming for the first time its typical form in the works of the German philosopher Hegel, was popularized in England by T. H. Green, and subsequently elaborated by the late Dr. Bosanquet, in whose book, *The Philosophical Theory of the State*, the most complete statement of the Absolutist Theory will be found.

In recent years the doctrine has been subjected on the theoretical side to searching criticism from a number of different points of view, while the semi-philosophical sanction which it has seemed to many to extend to the actual practice of States, especially in war time, has produced a sense of dissatisfaction with the theory, which has led men to seek in conceptions of a different order a substitute for the omnipotence of the Absolutist State. There is to-day, as we shall see in later chapters, a general bias against the State.

At the same time the theory is one of great importance on the philosophical side. It is consistently developed from the premises with which it starts, and it arrives at conclusions which, unless the premises themselves be questioned, it is difficult to refute.

It is proposed in the succeeding pages first to indicate the origins of the theory, secondly to state and describe the main positions adopted by those who hold it, and finally to outline the chief criticisms to which it has been subjected.

I. *Origins of the Absolutist Theory.*

The Absolutist theory of the State is derived from two rather different sources, both of which appear for the first time in Greek thought. In the first place there is a tendency to regard the State as a self-sufficing entity, identical with the whole of society. Thus Aristotle begins by abruptly announcing that it is the nature of the State to be self-sufficing, and Plato on the whole takes the same view. Where the existence of other States is specifically referred to, it is assumed that the only relation which they can have to the State is one of hostility. Thus, according to Greenidge, the natural or juristic relation of one Greek State to another was one of latent enmity, and was recognized as such. The philosopher Grotius held the doctrine of 'the freedom of the State from all external restraints', and Hobbes contents himself with the remark that 'States are by nature enemies'.

The State comes, therefore, to be discussed as though it were equivalent to the whole of human society, and what many thinkers regard as two distinct relationships, namely, the relationship of the individual as a citizen of a State to that State, and his relationship as a member of the human race to mankind as a whole, tend to be treated as if they were identical. Since the State is regarded as representing and containing within itself all the individual's social aspirations, and at the same time fulfilling all his social needs, whatever claims the State may make upon the individual are held to be based upon an absolute authority. In so far as the claims of associations other than the State are taken into account, it is assumed that the claims of the State must necessarily override them.

The Greek conception of human nature provides the starting point of the second line of thought which leads to the Absolutist State. Many writers on political theory have held that the real and essential nature of the individual is that which he possessed in some hypothetical State of Nature before he began to dwell in society. Society has in consequence been regarded as an artificial structure, imposed upon the natural and primitive state of man as the result of a definite contract into which individuals entered in order to put an end to the intolerable insecurity of the State of Nature. This theory of the origin of society is called the Social Contract Theory.

The Greek philosophers Plato and Aristotle advanced an entirely different view as to the nature both of man and of society. Beginning with the conception of man as a social or political animal, they argued that, from the very fact that he is social it is natural for him to live in society. The life of the individual isolated from his fellows is a life against nature, and the real nature of the individual can in consequence only be developed in society. It is only by living in society that a man can realize all that he has it in him to be, only by intercourse with his fellows, by the realization of social duties and the fulfilment of social obligations that he can develop his full self. In addition, therefore, to the obvious benefits of security against violence and redress against injustice that the individual receives from the State, he owes it a debt of gratitude for its bestowal upon him of his own individuality in all its richness and with all its potentialities.

II. *Statement of the Theory.*

The conception of the State as the guarantor, and in some sense the creator, of the real personality of the individual is extended and developed in the philosophy of Hegel. In his view men enjoy as members of society a freedom which is more real than that which they abandoned when they quitted their hypothetical lawless state of nature to enter society. This freedom, which became possible only in society, is an externalization or objectification of all that is highest in the conception of freedom in the individual's heart, a conception which but for society would remain unrealized. In the State, to use Hegel's language, man has fully raised his outward self to the level of his inward self of thought. This real freedom which exists in and is a product of society is active and developing. It manifests itself first in law, secondly in the rule of inward morality which the individual receives from society, and thirdly in the whole system of social institutions and influences that make for the development of personality.

The State thus makes possible for man a freedom to which he would otherwise be unable to attain. In Hegel's words, 'Nothing short of the State is the actualization of freedom'. But it only does this in virtue of the fact that the State is itself a real personality and has a real will. In representing, as it does, the wills of all its citizens who have contracted to live together in society, it causes to come into existence a new entity over and above the sum of the individual wills, which is the General Will, and a new personality over and above the sum of the individual personalities, which is the personality of the State; and it is in the General Will and in the personality of the State that the will and personality of each individual are made to transcend themselves.

As regards the General Will we may say that there always is such a will in regard to each question that arises for decision, although it may not find actual expression in action. Representing as it does that aspect of the individual's will which harmonizes with the wills of others, his will, that is to say, for the good of all, including self, as opposed to his will for the good of self at the expense of all, it is of necessity always rational and always right. It is in fact the transmuted and sublimated essence of what is best in the wills of all, but is sharply to be distinguished from the mere arithmetical sum of those wills. It is accordingly through the expression of his will in the General Will that the individual may externalize in reality the highest of which he is capable in thought. It follows, therefore, that the actions of the State, in so far as they proceed from the General Will, must always be irreproachably right in the sense that they represent what is best in individual wills.

As regards the personality of the State, it is clear that the State, being a real individual, may be regarded as an end in itself, possessing rights of its own which necessarily override in any apparent conflict the so-called rights of the individual. The use of the words 'so-called' is designed to draw attention to the fact that the individual can have no *real* rights which conflict with those of the State; this is because the *real* rights of the individual are not those which he has brought with him from some hypothetical pre-social state of society, but the rights to pursue and attain to certain real ends which his fully developed nature sets before him. But it is only his nature as a member of society, a nature which he owes to society, that desires to pursue these ends. Not only, therefore, is society responsible for the ends which the individual desires to pursue, but it confers the right to pursue them. But since the individual receives his rights from the State, he can have no rights which conflict with those of the State.

Summing up the line of argument derived from a consideration of the nature of the General Will, of the personality of the State, and of real rights, we may with Hegel regard the State as 'a self-conscious ethical substance and a self-knowing and self-actualizing individual'.

Three somewhat paradoxical results follow from this conception.

First, the State can never act unrepresentatively. Thus the policeman who arrests the burglar, and the magistrate who locks him up, are really expressing the burglar's real will to be arrested and locked up, the policeman and magistrate being the executive officials of a State which necessarily represents and expresses the real will of the burglar who is a member of it. Furthermore, since the freedom which man obtains in and through the State is a real and concrete freedom and, as such, opposed to the abstract and unreal freedom which he enjoys as an isolated individual, the burglar is acting freely when he is being marched to the police-station. There is in fact a complete identification between liberty and law, real liberty only being attained in and through obedience to the law.

In the second place, the relations which bind the individual not only to every other individual in the community, but also to the State as a whole, themselves form an integral part of the individual's personality. He would not be what he is without them, and he only is what he is because of them. It follows that he cannot act as an isolated individual but only as an integral part of the State, and that he cannot will with a purely individual will but only with a part of the State's will. Thus, according to Dr. Bosanquet, even in rebelling against the State, the individual does not rebel with a will which has a different source from the State's will, but with a will which he has obtained from the State, which is indeed continuous with the State's will; the State, in short, in times of rebellion is divided against itself.

Thirdly, the State contains within itself and represents the social morality of all its citizens. Just as the personalities of all the individuals in the State are transcended by and merged in the personality of the State, so the moral relations which each citizen has to each other citizen are merged in or transcended by the social morality which is vested in the State. But this does not mean that the State is itself moral, or that it is bound by moral relations in its actions. For moral relations imply two parties, and there can be no other party besides the State which is itself the sum of all parties. As regards the existence of other

States, of parties, that is to say, which are outside the State, this, as we have already seen, is ignored. Dr. Bosanquet gives expression to this line of thought in the words, 'the State has no determinate function in a larger community, but is itself the supreme community; the guardian of a whole world, but not a factor within an organized moral world', and sums it up in the blunt statement: 'It is hard to see how the State can commit theft or murder in the sense in which these are moral offences.'

From this it is but a step to the complete doctrine of the absolutism of the State. In theory at all times, and in practice in war time, it may exercise, and lawfully exercise, complete authority over the lives of its citizens. Nor is there any ground in theory or law for resistance to its decrees, for those over whom it exercises authority are not different from those who exercise it, and its decrees are inspired by the real wills of those who obey them, even when they obey unwillingly. In an emergency the State may do what it pleases, and as to what constitutes an emergency the State is to judge for itself. 'When need arises,' says Dr. Bosanquet, 'of which it, through constitutional methods, is the sole judge', the State may call upon its citizens to place their lives at its disposal. It is indeed in the omnipotence of the State in time of war that the theory finds its most striking logical development. 'The state of war', writes Hegel, 'shows the omnipotence of the State in its individuality; country and fatherland are then the power which convicts of nullity the independence of individuals.'

It is true that some English thinkers have declined to accept all the implications of the Absolutist theory, or have at any rate failed to apply them with the ruthless logic of the German writers Bernhardi and Treitschke. Thus T. H. Green, who was an exponent of the theory of real rights described above, held that among other rights the individual possessed a 'right to life'. This right was clearly threatened by the doctrine of the absolute and unquestioned authority of the State in time of war, and Green concluded accordingly that war could at most be relatively right and never absolutely right. War is not for him an attribute of the perfect State, but of a particular State in its imperfect actuality. Green does not appear, however, to have attempted to solve the question which immediately presents itself, whether the individual is entitled to judge of any particular war, that it is not in a sufficient degree 'relatively right' to justify him in endangering the *real* 'right to life' of himself and others by taking part in it; nor to have faced the further question of the extent to which the State may override the 'right of life' of the resisting individual who judges a war to be relatively wrong.

Apart, however, from modifications which some English writers have, perhaps not very consistently, introduced into the theory, its general tendency is sufficiently clear. The State is the natural, necessary, and final form of human organization. In its perfect development it is both omnipotent and absolute, and all existing States are only States in so far as they partake of the State in its perfect development. The respects in which they fall short of the omnipotent State are to be deprecated, so that what we want is not less of the State but more. The State has furthermore a real will and a real personality of its own, which, from the very fact that they have derived from what is best in the personalities and wills of individuals, come to be endowed, if not with moral, at least with quasi-divine attributes. Thus the State in virtue both of its transcendent character and of the devotion and sacrifice which it imposes upon its members, enlarges their personalities, purging them of petty aims and human selfishness; 'it carries back', says Hegel, 'the individual, whose tendency it is to become a centre of his own, into the life of the universal substance'.

And to the obvious objection that no State that has ever

existed exercises any of these functions, the Absolutist replies that he is not describing the practice of existing States, but the attributes of the ideal State; and that it is quite natural for him to do this, since only the ideal State is really and truly a State, all other States, in so far as they fall short of the ideal State, being to that extent not States.

III. *Criticisms of the Theory.*

As we shall have occasion to point out in succeeding chapters, there has been a marked reaction in recent political thought from the Absolutist philosophy of the State. It is denounced as unsound in theory, untrue to fact, and liable to extend a dangerous sanction to the more unscrupulous actions of existing States in the sphere of foreign policy. This reaction has in some quarters proceeded to the length of a complete denial of the necessity for the existence of the State, or indeed of any equivalent repository for sovereignty in the community. It is proposed briefly to consider first the theoretical objections which are brought against the theory, and secondly the facts of which it fails in the view of its critics to take account.

A. *Theoretical objections.* The assumption of the identity of the State with the sum total of human society, which is obviously false in fact, vitiates a number of conclusions which unconsciously involve this assumption. Thus, even if the claim of the State to complete omnipotence in respect of its relations with its own citizens be admitted, it is clear that this claim can only be sustained on the assumption that the State represents and transcends in its own will the wills of all the individuals who compose it. Now there is no suggestion that the State represents the wills of citizens belonging to other States: it is not, therefore, omnipotent in respect of them. Since the claim to omnipotence is used to justify the further claim to exemption from moral obligations, it follows that the exemption does not in any event extend to the relations between the State and other States. The State in its relationship with other States is assuredly *not* 'the guardian of a whole world' and *is* 'a factor within an organized moral world'. It follows that the State has no more justification for non-moral action in its dealings with other States than has a voluntary association, other than the State, in its dealings with other such associations.

If in fact the principle of morality be recognized as a possible guiding principle in the relations of one individual with another, there is no reason why it should suddenly cease to be acknowledged as a guiding principle in the relations of a number or group of individuals with another group. Once this is granted it becomes difficult to see why it is any harder for the State 'to commit theft or murder in the sense in which these are moral offences' than it is for a church or a trading company to do the same.

But is the case materially different as regards the relationship of the State to its own members? We may grant the proposition that it is participation in society which alone enables a man to develop his full nature, and that it is only in society therefore that he can be really free. The castaway on a desert island also enjoys freedom, but it is an abstract freedom in the sense that, though he is at liberty to do whatever he can, there is practically nothing that he can do. But the admission of this principle does not necessarily carry with it an admission of the omnipotence of the State. The State exists for individuals; individuals do not exist for the State. Liberty has meaning only for the individual, and the welfare of society and the State has neither meaning nor value unless it carries with it the welfare of the individuals who compose the State. In other words, the State and the community are not ends in themselves.

Once this is realized, it becomes clear that any theory of the State which admits the possibility that the welfare of the State may be achieved, apart from or at the expense of the happiness of individuals, and justifies its admission on the ground that the personality of the State contains and transcends that of the individual, is, in effect, putting the cart before the horse. Nor is it legitimate to meet this criticism, as supporters of the theory do, with the contention that it is not possible for the State to promote its welfare at the expense of that of the individual, or even to tyrannize over the individual, since the welfare of the State is that of the individual, and the will of the State, even when tyrannizing, is the will of the individuals who are the victims of the tyranny. A decision does not become my personal decision because it is carried against my will and vote by an association of which I am a member. By the mere fact of living together in a State men do not cause a social miracle to take place whereby their will is transformed into its direct opposite by the operation of democracy, any more than an equivalent miracle is performed when a minority is outvoted on the committee of a cricket club.

Nor is there any substance in a distinction between a 'real' will of which I may be unaware and a so-called unreal will of which I am ordinarily aware, the alleged 'real' will being defined as a will to carry out every decision of the majority of an association to which I belong, although what I am in fact aware of is a conviction that the decisions in question are wrong. It is difficult to escape the conclusion that the attribution of a 'real' will to the individual which is necessarily and always in accord with the general will in which it is merged, is only a device for giving an appearance of justice and democracy to what must otherwise appear the purely arbitrary and tyrannical acts of a sovereign State. The Absolutist theory of the State is in fact inimical to individual freedom, because, whenever a conflict occurs between an individual and the State, it takes the view that the latter must inevitably be right.

By throwing doubt on the view that the wills of the individual and the State are always identical, it is not intended to suggest that they are always opposed. The question that demands solution is not how to strike a balance between the claims and counterclaims of the individual and society, but how to decide what amount and what kind of organization will secure to the individual the greatest amount of personal liberty.

B. *Practical considerations.* As soon as the problem is stated in this way, it becomes necessary for the theorist to take into account the enormous growth in the number of voluntary associations formed for special purposes which has characterized the last half-century. These associations are mainly of two kinds; associations of individuals for economic purposes and associations of individuals for ethical purposes.

The growth of associations for economic purposes has been fostered by the increased facilities for communication, which have, from the economic point of view, constituted the civilized world one social unit. Though politically divided into a number of independent nation States, human society now exemplifies on the economic side that organic interdependence which the Idealist theory asserts to be of the essence of the State on the political side; the economic welfare of any part of it is, that is to say, dependent upon the welfare of the rest. 'The telegraph', says Norman Angell, 'involves a single system of credit for the civilized world; that system of credit involves the financial interdependence of all States.'

The effect of the growth of economic associations is seen in the substitution of economic bonds based on community of interest in money making, for the old national bonds based on the chances of birth in the same square mile, which previously formed the chief if not the only foundation for human association. In the society of to-day the individual member of a company whose object is the production and importation of oranges from Brazil has a greater interest in the efficiency and prosperity of the Brazilians, who produce and export the oranges, than in the welfare of his next-door neighbour in a London suburb, whom he probably does not know and might very well dislike if he did.

Such a change in the character of the factors determining human association, and the consequent change in the direction of the individual's interests, may be said at least to foreshadow the possibility of an organization of society based on economic affinities as an alternative to the existing division based on territorial proximities.

The case of associations for ethical purposes is not dissimilar. As the result of the Individualist thinking of the nineteenth century there is a general tendency to abandon the moral theory of the Greeks that there is only one, or at most two or three kinds of good life for the individual, which it is the business of the State to promote. We hold, on the contrary, that there may be an indefinite number of different conceptions of the good life, varying as the natures of individuals vary, and that it is essential that the choice between these various conceptions should rest with the individual. It is only through individuals that the vague aspirations and religious insight of any age gain expression, and spontaneity in matters of conduct and belief is accordingly of much greater importance than uniformity.

The increasing strain and complexity of modern life have produced a corresponding complexity of religious needs. These needs no longer find satisfaction in a single State-controlled Church, and issue accordingly in a bewildering variety of associations for ethical and religious purposes, which, in common with the economic associations already referred to, pay no attention to political State boundaries but, like the Theosophical Society, the Roman Catholic Church, or the Christian Science organization, embrace citizens belonging to numbers of different States.

Under the influence of these associations men tend to substitute a private morality of their own for the conventional morality prescribed by the State, and, as a consequence, to question on moral grounds any attempt on the part of the State to interfere with the pursuit of the good life as they conceive it. Social life, especially as it expresses itself in politics, frequently observes a lower standard of morality than that which men maintain in private. Mere outward observance of the State laws does not demand a high degree of morality, so that a law-abiding citizen is not necessarily a moral man, while a law-making citizen is not infrequently an immoral man.

In these circumstances it is not surprising that, where there is a conflict of claims on a question involving moral issues, the individual should not only demand the right to decide for himself, but should tend and tend increasingly to put the claims of his voluntary association whether economic or ethical before those of the State.

We may then conclude that the Idealist theory of the State ignores certain important facts, when it asserts, in Professor Bosanquet's words, that the State will undoubtedly, ' when need arises of which it, through constitutional methods, is the sole judge, prohibit and prevent the expression in external acts of any loyalty but that to the community which it represents '.

In particular it ignores the fact that voluntary bodies of the kind described now embrace all that is most intimate in the individual's life, that every activity that fills his pocket or enriches his soul is now carried out in associations non-coterminous with the State, and that these associations imply, and in fact create, a stratification of society different from and opposed to the State division based on geographical boundaries.

Despite the vast increase in the external activities of the State during the first decade of the twentieth century, it was, nevertheless, in fact being squeezed out of the life of the individual. So much was this the case that the ordinary individual was only brought into contact with the State organization when he had to pay taxes, to serve on a jury, or to vote, functions of comparatively infrequent occurrence and limited appeal. It follows that a political philosophy which endeavours to embrace within its scope the existence of associations other than the State, to estimate the bearing of these associations upon the State, to strike a balance between their conflicting claims and to apportion their respective functions, is more closely in accord with the facts of society than the Idealist tendency to contemplate the State as an isolated, self-sufficient entity, which must of necessity remain unaffected by any apparently external relations to voluntary associations, since the fact of these relations is comprehended in its all-embracing structure.

The reaction from the Absolutist theory of the State assumes one of two forms. Either the theory of the General Will and the real personality of the State is admitted, but admitted only to be extended to groups and associations of individuals other than the State; or the General Will and real personality are bluntly denied as metaphysical figments, the State being reduced to a mere piece of administrative machinery, which may one day be scrapped and superseded by a complex of voluntary associations.

The hostile attitude to the State which underlies both these forms of reaction expresses itself in various ways in most of the different theories whose consideration forms the subject of the remainder of this book. On the whole the prevailing tendency is to insist on the real being and personality of groups, and, in the next chapter as well as in the chapter on Guild Socialism, we shall be concerned with the attempt to transfer to such groups formed on a voluntary basis many of the functions claimed by the Absolutists for the State.

2

Modern Individualism

Introductory.

INDIVIDUALISM regarded as a social and political theory was a product of the nineteenth century. First enunciated in its nineteenth-century form by Bentham and James Mill, it received its fullest expression about the middle of the century in the works of John Stuart Mill and Herbert Spencer. From 1880 onwards its authority began to wane, and by the end of the century it had been largely superseded by the Absolutist theory of the State.

A book, therefore, such as the present, which seeks to provide an introduction to modern political theory, is not, strictly speaking, required to give an account of the Individualism of the Victorian age. At the same time it will be desirable briefly to outline the main features of nineteenth-century Individualism, in order that modern Individualism may be seen in its true perspective, and the legitimacy of its descent from the older theory established.

Nineteenth-century Individualism. The most characteristic statement of nineteenth-century Individualism is to be found in the works of John Stuart Mill, entitled *On Liberty* and *Representative Government.* Mill, in common with other Utilitarian thinkers, is in revolt against the political abstractions which subsequently reached their full development in the theory considered in the last chapter. He insists on regarding every political question in terms of the happiness or unhappiness of human beings, and not, as did the lawyers and the Hegelians, in terms of an abstraction such as the General Will or the personality of the State. While conceding, therefore, the contention of the Absolutists that, since the State is a natural growth or organism, it is only in the State that the individual can enjoy the fullest

JOHN STUART MILL

happiness of which his nature is capable, he goes on to point out that this admission does not mean that the State does not exist for the happiness of individuals. He then proceeds to draw the conclusion that it is the business of Government actively to promote the happiness of individuals, and that, if it fails in this respect, it must give way to some other form of social organization that succeeds.

Now Mill's main thesis is that the State can best further the happiness of individuals by interfering in their personal affairs as little as possible. This is particularly the case in the sphere of opinion. Mill's essay *On Liberty* is perhaps the most famous vindication of freedom of thought, and the most powerful plea for the toleration of opinions we fail to understand, in the whole of literature. He insisted upon the extension of this freedom to 'cranks', on the ground that, while nine cranks out of ten are harmless idiots, the tenth is of greater value to mankind than all the normal men who seek to suppress him. Such a one is defended by Mill not only against State interference and suppression, but also against the persecution of orthodox public opinion. Mill has a peculiar horror of the mob mind, of the tyranny of the crowd drugged by the poison of the ambitious vulgarians whose privately owned press forms its prejudices and moulds its outlook, of the perversion of the public school spirit which countenances the torture of a defenceless new boy because of the number of buttons on his coat or the sound of his surname.

His contention is that the fact that public opinion is strongly opposed to certain views does not in the least mean (subject to the proviso mentioned below) that the Government is entitled to suppress those who hold them. For, since it is the business of Government to promote happiness, and, since happiness means the happiness of individuals, it is clear that Government is not justified in infringing the happiness of minorities by suppressing their views, even when it is backed by a compact majority of men holding the contrary views. 'Mankind', said Mill, 'are greater gainers by suffering each other to live as seems good to themselves, than by compelling each to live as seems good to the rest.'

But to vindicate liberty of thought is a comparatively easy task. What is at once more important and more difficult is the establishment of the right to expression of individuality in freedom of conduct. Freedom of conduct Mill calls 'one of the principal ingredients of human happiness, and quite the chief ingredient of individual and social progress'. Mill claims complete freedom of conduct for the individual in all matters not affecting the community. In matters which do affect the community, the community has a right to coerce the individual if his conduct is prejudicial to its welfare. This right of coercion on the part of the community in matters affecting its welfare constitutes the proviso referred to above, to which Mill's vindication of freedom of thought is also subject.

Mill has been severely criticized for the distinction which his principle implies between self-regarding actions and actions which affect other people. Critics have laboriously pointed out that the line between these two classes of actions is one which it is impossible to draw, and that, since we are all members of one society, all our actions must necessarily affect in some degree the other members of that society. But Mill was not a fool, and he did not suppose that his distinction could be applied with mathematical precision. It was sufficient for him that it afforded a rough and ready guide of considerable utility, and that, in affirming the principle that freedom of conduct should be the rule unless good cause could be shown to the contrary, it corrected the adverse balance against the individual created by the theories described in the previous chapter. By identifying the 'real freedom' of the individual with action in conformity with the State's will, these theories imply a false distinction between an individual's apparent freedom of which he is aware and which he enjoys, and his ' real ' freedom of which he is unaware and which the State enjoys. Individualists, moreover, have often pointed out that, even if the claim to infallibility advanced on behalf of the State were in theory to be accepted, it is clear that in practice the State is often far from infallible. In practice the State is a collection of officials and inspectors, sometimes wise, sometimes foolish, with no more claim to omniscience than the individuals they propose to coerce ; and Mill makes it sufficiently clear that any theory which claims on behalf of these officers that they know what is good for the individual, or what constitutes his freedom, better than he does himself, is absurd.

Mill's Individualism, therefore, issues in the general conclusion that the State will do well to leave people alone so long as the people in question leave other people alone. Stated thus, Individualism is a doctrine that cannot but command respect. Resting as it does upon a sound basis, it rises to an expression of the highest political aspirations of which men are capable. All men at bottom regard Government as a necessary nuisance. We are all Anarchists at times, and the Anarchist doctrine, when we come to consider it in detail, will be found to be little more than an elaboration of the claim for full individual freedom which Mill formulated, a denial of the sovereignty which he recognized as inherent in the State, and a refusal to admit the importance of the necessary distinction between self-regarding and other-regarding actions.

Apart, however, from the difficulty of giving effect to this distinction in practice, the Individualism of the nineteenth century suffered from two very serious drawbacks, which set the current against Individualistic theory for thirty or forty years. It is, in fact, only in very recent years that Individualism has shown signs of renewed vitality, and it is this modern version of Individualism, a version which, inspired by the spirit of Mill, seeks to safeguard his doctrine from the dangers to which it is exposed, that it is proposed to consider in this chapter. First, however, we must consider the drawbacks which led men to abandon in practice much of the teaching of the old Individualism.

Objections to Nineteenth-century Individualism.

(1) Herbert Spencer gave to Mill's Individualism a new complexion by importing into it biological conceptions derived from the Darwinian doctrine of evolution. While regarding the State as contractual in origin, like a limited liability company, he also believed somewhat inconsistently in the theory of society as an organism which has evolved. In this organism those members who are not fitted to play their part must be eliminated in the interests of the whole, and it is not, therefore, the business of the other members to perpetuate their weakness by making provision for it. Arguing from the Darwinian phrase, 'the survival of the fittest', Spencer is thus led to denounce all forms of State relief to the poor and all collective effort on behalf of the distressed. Progress consists for him in the elimination of those who fall behind in the struggle for existence. This development of the gentler creed of Mill implied a reversion to the ethics of barbarism, and not only discredited Individualism in the eyes of socially minded men, but had particularly important consequences in the economic sphere.

(2) It was more particularly in this sphere that Individualism proved inadequate to the needs of the times. The doctrine of liberty, of which the importance cannot be overestimated in politics, worked disastrously when applied in the field of economics.

Bentham had held that, since men were fundamentally selfish, each man could be trusted to look after his own interests. The doctrine that a man knew what he wanted better than any one else, and would pursue what he wanted with more energy and persistence than any one would pursue it for him, found expression in the belief that no outside interference was either desirable or necessary in the dealings between man and man. This social theory wedded to the political economy of the times gave birth to the complete doctrine of *laissez faire*. Proceeding upon the basis of what they believed to be the teaching of political economy, Individualists now held that in the economic sphere outside interference in the dealings between man and man was not only undesirable, but also and necessarily ineffective. The iron Law of Wages, the iron Law of Supply and Demand, and other shibboleths culled from the text-books of political economists, were held to prove that any artificial adjustment by the State in matters affecting wages and output must inevitably be nullified by the operation of automatically determining forces. A policy which left men to bargain with one another unhindered and unchecked was, therefore, not only consonant with the doctrine of individual liberty, but was necessitated by the nature of things.

While from the political point of view the doctrine of *laissez faire* has much to commend it—a policy of non-interference is clearly preferable to a universal meddling with everybody's affairs with the State poking its inspectors into every household—in the economic sphere it produced the disastrous consequences from which, more than from any other factor, the various theories of Socialism, to be described in succeeding chapters, derive the strength of their appeal. It produced these consequences because it rested upon three serious fallacies:

(*a*) That each individual is equally far-sighted and has an equal capacity for knowing what he wants.

(*b*) That each individual possesses an equal power of obtaining what he wants, and an equal freedom of choice.

(*c*) That the satisfaction of the wants of all individuals is identical with the well-being of the community as a whole.

The refusal of the dominant school of Manchester Individualism to recognize these fallacies made of nineteenth-century Individualism a competitive struggle for the means of existence.

But the maxim, 'Every man for himself and the Devil take the hindmost,' does not afford an adequate basis for a contented society, and the distress occasioned by its practical application led to a policy of State interference in industrial and economic processes, which was, indeed, only one aspect of that growing activity of the State in all departments of public life which characterized the early years of the twentieth century.

This growth in the functions of the State was due in part to the dominance of the philosophy of the State already described, in part to the propaganda of the Collectivist Socialists which will form the subject of our next chapter. But the reaction against Individualism has produced a reaction in its turn. The wheel has turned full circle, and the present dissatisfaction with the State has promoted a revival of Individualist thinking akin in spirit though not in form to the Individualism of the nineteenth century.

Factors promoting the growth of Modern Individualism.

(1) Although the State has multiplied its functions in every department of public life, it has nevertheless been progressively eliminated from the private life of the individual. The growth of voluntary associations for economic and ethical purposes already described has tended to make men think of the State as just one, and not always the most important one, of the various bodies to which the individual may belong. It has not necessarily the first claim on his allegiance, and it certainly does not always command the warmest of his sympathies. The State after all, with the possible exception of the family, is the only association which a man joins not from choice but from necessity. He chooses to belong to his football club or his Trade Union; he is born into his State.

(2) The enormous extension of Governmental activity in all belligerent countries during the war has produced a feeling of

hostility to the State as such. Just because the calls which the State has made upon the individual have been more exacting, the individual is more inclined to dispute the grounds on which they are made. He is the readier to do this because of the growing tendency in some quarters to attribute the fact of war itself to the predatory power exercised by the modern State, combined with its irresponsibility in the sphere of external relations, an irresponsibility justified, as we have seen, by the Hegelian theory of the State. At the same time the assumption by the State of new powers in internal affairs, and the consequent curtailment of the liberty of the individual, the increase in the number of officials and in the scope of their authority, have given people a disagreeable foretaste of the kind of Government which the existence of an efficient bureaucracy in a highly organized State would involve.

(3) The war and the psychology of war-time have also given rise to a quickened apprehension of the dangers of majority rule. The individual feels that he needs to be protected against the mob mind, crushing with the intolerance born of homogeneity all spontaneity and innovation in the protestant or detached minority. The integration of social forces caused by the pressure of population, and the growing weight of a public opinion at once formed by and mirrored in a popular press, have seemed to threaten a tyranny of mass rule which would preclude the possibility of that untrammelled individual development which Mill so rightly valued. It has become important, therefore, to evolve a political theory which would recognize in the first place that the transfer of legal sovereignty to the majority of the moment under the name of the State is no guarantee of universal happiness, and would endeavour in the second, by dispersing the powers and functions of the State over as wide an area as possible, to afford the individual some protection against the mass.

Modern Individualism. The various lines of thought which we have grouped together under the name of 'Modern Individualism', however much they may differ in other respects, exhibit a common endeavour to provide the basis for such a theory.

(1) The views put forward in Mr. Norman Angell's *The Great Illusion* obtained considerable notoriety in the years preceding the war. They have subsequently been shown to be untrue in certain particulars, but they have been more often misrepresented than disproved. Mr. Angell's main contention is that men are united by a community of feeling based on economic interests which not only runs counter to but frequently transcends national and geographical boundaries. The essence of this community of feeling lies in the fact that, on the whole, people always do what pays them best. At present they often take wrong views of what does pay them owing to the deliberate misrepresentation of issues and fostering of nationalist feeling by competing States. But Mr. Angell points to the obvious fact that 'It pays men better to think and feel as members of the universal, economic society whose attribute is peace, than to think and feel as members of limited political societies whose attribute is war'.

Men cannot fail indefinitely to recognize this fact. When they do recognize it, they will discard the present division of society into competing nationalist groups for an economic stratification based on considerations of what is profitable. Nor is this development to be regretted. People who act wisely as individuals act like fools as citizens, and the world suffers in consequence. Mr. Angell speaks sadly of 'The fact that a man will in politics, in a matter where patriotism is involved, act with an irrationalism and an absence of any sense of responsibility, which he would never display in the conduct of his private business'. It is not surprising to find that Mr. Angell regards the State as merely a piece of administrative mechanism. It can be superseded and transferred to the evolutionary scrap heap so soon as machinery better calculated to advance men's interests has been devised.

We may therefore look forward to a period when the national State is merged in an international order of society based on an economic class basis.

This development may, it is true, result in the substitution of a class war between different economic strata for a patriotic war between different national units; but it will at least provide men with an organization of society which fulfils and expresses the real needs of the individual, instead of misrepresenting or stifling them. And if the prospect of fighting in class wars instead of in national wars fails to allure, an indication of a better way is perhaps to be found in the theories of the Guild Socialists. These theories accept all that is sound in Mr. Angell's criticism of the State, but differ from him in outlining an organization of society which, while curtailing the functions of the State, would substitute co-operation for conflict in the economic sphere.

(2) Based upon a similar distrust of the power of the over-developed State but issuing in conclusions very unlike those of Mr. Angell, Mr. Graham Wallas's *Great Society* concerns itself mainly with the problem of representative Government. The transference of the means of production from private to social ownership, advocated by the Socialists, is of no value unless the public body that is to administer them is really representative of the society that owns them. And the question arises for Mr. Wallas whether the modern centralized State with Parliament as its organ of expression does in fact produce the most vigorous 'collective mind'.

The machinery of election in a centralized State administered by a governing body elected on a geographical basis is liable to very serious defects which may prevent it from giving adequate expression to what is best as opposed to what is worst in the popular will. The electorate may be hypnotized by the popular press, drugged with advertisements, deafened by the 'boosting' of so-called business candidates. It may be influenced, as in the case of the 1918 elections, by centralized mass suggestion, exercised through all the organs which form and control public opinion, into condoning and even encouraging a policy of hatred and passion of which each individual would in his private capacity be ashamed. It may be suborned by powerful financial groups into voting for measures which though prejudicial to the common welfare are advantageous to the groups in question.

All these are dangers which beset in a peculiar degree large bodies voting in masses for the purpose of electing representatives they do not know to a remote Chamber upon which, thereafter, they exercise no control.

Mr. Wallas, accordingly, proposes that the electorate should be divided into groups on a vocational basis, and that each group should elect members to a Second Chamber which would be composed entirely of representatives of the different trades and professions. A lower Chamber would be retained elected on a purely geographical basis. Another proposal is for the election of bodies of representatives on a geographical basis for the carrying out of particular undertakings, leavened by a minority of members appointed by professional organizations. Throughout these proposals Mr. Wallas's object is to secure that the individual shall be safeguarded against the evils of unrestricted majority rule. It is not so much the oppression of the State as the tyranny of the mob mind that is the object of apprehension.

(3) Certain suggestions in favour of a return to the Medieval Guild, put forward by Mr. Belloc in a book entitled *The Servile State*, have been developed by the Guild Socialists, who tend to regard society as a federation of two kinds of groups, representing respectively the producers' and the consumers' point of view. The existing Trade Unions and Co-operative Societies are taken as the germ from which this group organization of society will be developed. The proposals of the Guild Socialists, which constitute, perhaps, the most typical illustration of the attitude of

modern Individualists, will be considered later in a separate chapter.

The above brief outline will serve to indicate some of the main features of the political tendency which we have termed Modern Individualism. They may be summarized as follows:

(1) A disposition to anti-intellectualism directed in general against the State and in particular against the Hegelian and Collectivist theories of the State. This anti-intellectualism expresses itself in a hostility to concrete reasoned proposals, in a belief that the future will develop along its own lines unaffected by the cerebrations of statesmen and of political theorists, and in a faith in the ability of instinct or the subconscious to grapple successfully with each new situation as and when it arises. Syndicalism affords a typical expression of this attitude. In general the State is either discredited on moral grounds or subordinated to other forms of association on economic grounds.

(2) An affirmation of the real personality of groups. It is urged that the arguments used by Hegelians to establish the existence of a State personality over and above the personalities of the individuals composing the State, and of a Common Will which is different both from the sum total and from the mechanical resultant of the wills of all, will, if valid for the State, apply with equal validity to the group. The Trade Union, the College, the Church Guild, and even the football club, possess equally with the State a personality created by the consenting wills of their members, and are accordingly entitled to call upon their loyalty and service. When, as may sometimes happen, this loyalty conflicts with a man's allegiance to his State, there is no *a priori* reason derived from the nature of things or of States, why the State's claims should be regarded as necessarily paramount. In any event it is essential that the choice between conflicting claims should lie entirely within the individual's discretion.

(3) The State tends to be regarded as little more than a federa-

tion of groups, a union of Guilds, or a 'community of communities', a piece of administrative machinery useful for co-ordinating activities and adjusting claims between conflicting groups, but not in itself responding to any unique and peculiar need of the human spirit which is capable of being satisfied by no other form of organization.

A State so regarded might cease to be indispensable, so soon as the group organization of society, which, it is suggested, might replace it, had perfected the necessary machinery for regulating cases in which the interests of the groups overlapped.

Thus the New Individualism differs from the old in regarding the group and not the individual as its unit for political purposes. It has been driven to take this view by the necessity for which the old Individualism failed to provide, of protecting the individual human being against exploitation and oppression by the power of (1) privately owned economic interests, and (2) public opinion expressing itself in the rule of the majority. The group is organized in the first place for protection, and in the second for the furtherance of certain interests or ideas which its members have in common. Owing to its comparative smallness it affords opportunities for the expression of the Common Will and the development of individual personality, which the size of the State precludes.

It is urged on behalf of the group, therefore, that it has not only succeeded to function, originally attributed to the State, of developing the real personality of the individual, but that it is the only effective guarantee of that personal liberty, concern for which forms the most valuable element of the old Individualism as expounded by Mill.

A detailed description of proposals for a group organization of society will be given in the chapter on Guild Socialism.

3

Socialism: with special reference to Collectivism

Introductory.

It is a matter of some difficulty to give within a small compass a comprehensive account of Socialism. This difficulty is due in the first place to the fact that the word 'Socialism' is used to denote both a body of doctrine and a political movement, so that, although we shall be chiefly concerned with Socialist doctrine, it is not possible altogether to exclude from our account references to the nature of the various organizations which profess it. In the second place the body of doctrine which may be roughly termed Socialism is by no means wholly or even mainly political; it is to a large extent economic, and economic and political theories are in any event so closely interwoven, that it is not practicable nor even desirable to confine our description solely to the political aspects of Socialism.

A third difficulty arises from the fact that Socialists are divided into a number of opposing schools, which are separated by acute differences both as regards their aims and their methods. These schools are in some cases sufficiently important, and the peculiar doctrines for which they stand are sufficiently well defined, for their supporters to be known by separate and distinctive names; they are not Socialists, but Syndicalists, Guild Socialists, or Communists. These developments of Socialism will be considered in separate chapters. Descriptions of Socialism will, moreover, vary considerably according to the angle of approach. We may, for example, consider Socialism mainly as a reaction from Individualism; or we may treat it as an exposition of the theories of Karl Marx. Each method of treatment will emphasize different aspects of Socialism, and will result in the presentation of a different picture. More perhaps than any other theory, Socialism proves to be a different creed in the hands of each of its exponents, varying with the temperaments of its advocates and the nature of the abuses which have prompted their advocacy. As the advocates of Socialism are very numerous, and many of them have been first-rate political pamphleteers, the literature of the subject is enormous, with the result that it is hard to say in what exactly it is that Socialism consists. Socialism, in short, is like a hat that has lost its shape because everybody wears it.

At the same time there are a certain number of ends which most Socialists regard as desirable, however much they may differ as to the means by which they are to be attained. There is also a certain school of Socialist thought, which may be entitled Collectivist or State Socialism, which, though it has of recent years lost favour, constitutes at once a central body of doctrine and a point of departure for other theories.

It is then with this general basis of agreement, more particularly as it is embodied in Collectivist or State Socialism, that we shall be concerned in the present chapter.

It is proposed first to consider the antecedents of Socialism, then to give an account of the social and political philosophy which underlies it, and finally to describe some of the concrete proposals in which it finds expression. We shall so far as possible select those proposals to which, with minor modifications, Socialists of every school would assent.

I. *Antecedents of Collectivist Socialism.*

A. *The work of Karl Marx.* Karl Marx is in a very real sense the father of Socialism.[1] Before Marx there had, of course, been

[1] This statement requires qualification as regards some aspects of British Socialism. Marx is the point of departure for practically all continental Socialists and for some British Socialists. For others, however, and in particular for the Fabians, Hodgskin, Owen, and Ruskin are more important as antecedents.

numerous theorists who, dissatisfied with the existing state of society, had found vent for their dissatisfaction in planning ideal Utopias in which property was held in common and injustice was unknown. Plato's Republic may be termed a Socialist State in this sense. Some, like Robert Owen, had even attempted to give their ideals concrete expression, by the formation of model communities whose inhabitants were required to live the particular kind of life which the founder of the community considered to be the best life for man. These experiments were, however, without exception, failures; nor can it be said that, with the possible exception of Owen, the so-called Socialist writers before Marx paid any serious attention either to the question how their ideal state of society was to be realized, or to the further question how, when it had been realized, its continued working could be made practicable. Most of them, with the sublime confidence of the inspired social theorist, appear to have thought with Owen and Fourier that they had only to draw the attention of mankind to the obvious perfection of their schemes, when mankind would be automatically seized with an all-compelling desire to put them into practice. It is needless to say that the lives of most Utopian theorists have been full of disappointment.

Marx, then, is the first Socialist writer whose work can be termed scientific. He not only sketched the kind of society which he desired, but spoke in detail of the stages through which it must evolve.

Marx's writings, despite the great influence they have exercised over the working classes, are by no means free from difficulty, and there is considerable controversy as to the correct interpretation which should be placed upon them. The different interpretations of which they are susceptible have in part become, as we shall see, the points of departure for different schools of Socialists.

It will be sufficient for our present purpose to describe the two leading doctrines of Marx, leaving their developments to later chapters. These are the Theory of Value, and the Materialistic conception of History.

(1) *The Theory of Surplus Value.* Marx accepts in its entirety the doctrine which embodies the orthodox economics of the nineteenth century, that labour is the source of value, develops it, and then bases upon it conclusions which are almost the exact antithesis of those drawn by the economists. The Theory as Marx states it is as follows :

The wealth of capitalist societies is in the last resort an enormous collection of commodities. These commodities have value, the value being proportionate to their capacity for supplying human wants, or, in other words, to their usefulness. We assess the amount of 'usefulness' that an object possesses by finding out what it can be exchanged for, and Marx accordingly uses the words 'exchange-value' to denote the worth of an article in terms of its relation to other articles. This 'exchange-value', commonly represented by 'price', may fluctuate according to market conditions, but these fluctuations are accidental and do not eliminate or even obscure the real influence which determines both the value and, ultimately, the 'exchange-value' of commodities. This influence is the average amount of labour-time spent in the production of the commodity. Thus the labour-time which is socially necessary for the production of commodities asserts itself 'like an over-riding law of nature' in spite of superficial variations in exchange-values, as the real standard or measure of exchange-value.

But human labour cannot by itself create value ; it must use instruments without which it cannot work. These instruments are machinery, factories, steam power, electrical power, and so forth.

As the result of the inventions of the late eighteenth and early nineteenth centuries, these instruments for the creation of value have been enormously increased both in number and in efficiency, and are owned by a relatively small class, the capitalist class. The capitalist buys the labour power of the destitute workman, applies it to the machinery and raw materials which he owns, and as a result produces a commodity having 'exchange value', that is, a commodity which can be sold for a price which is greater than the amount expended in the payment of the workmen's wages and the upkeep of the factory. This difference between the exchange value of the manufactured commodity and the price paid to the workman for his labour is called Surplus Value. It is brought into being by the labour of the workman, and appropriated by the capitalist who employs him; it is in fact the product of unpaid labour.

This appropriation of Surplus Value by the capitalist constitutes the fundamental injustice of the modern industrial system, an injustice which all forms of Socialism seek to remove. The capitalist industrial system is, in fact, different only in form from a slave society. The slave worked and created surplus value under compulsion; the modern workman creates surplus value under a free contract into which he voluntarily enters. But inasmuch as the workman is unprovided with the means of production, he has, in fact, no alternative but to sell the one commodity he possesses, namely, his labour, to the capitalist, who after paying him a bare subsistence wage pockets the proceeds.

(2) *The Materialist Conception of History.* Marx then proceeds to inquire how society came to be organized in such a way that a small privileged class persistently appropriates the surplus value created by the labour of the workers under the protection of the law. His answer to this question is afforded by the Materialist Conception of History. Marx was the first to emphasize the decisive importance of economic factors in determining historical events. Where others had explained these events as the outcome

of personal ambition, court intrigue, or political aggression, Marx insisted on the fact that economic considerations would be found in the long run to underlie and to determine all apparently political tendencies. On this interpretation of history it would be not Menelaus' desire to be revenged upon Paris for eloping with Helen that took the Greeks to Troy, but the determination of the Greeks to open a new trade route to the East. History, then, is determined in the long run by the interplay of economic forces ; and the evolution of human society will at each stage reflect the stage of material development reached in the external world.

Thus to each stage of economic production there corresponds an appropriate political form and an appropriate class structure. The enormous economic advance caused by the Industrial Revolution at the beginning of the nineteenth century has called into being first, a small privileged class, the owners of the means of production, second, a large propertyless proletariat. There had, of course, been employers and workers before the Industrial Revolution ; there had even been small-scale capitalists, but what is peculiar about modern society is the dominance of the capitalists as a class, the organization of the State so as to give expression to that dominance, and the confrontation of the capitalists all along the economic line by the proletariat. This hostile confrontation, with the fundamental opposition of interests it implies, gives rise to the perpetual struggle and conflict which is called 'the class war'.

But society is not static ; it changes and evolves, and the capitalist stage in its evolution will in due course pass away and be succeeded by another. The future development of capitalism will take the form of the concentration of capital into fewer and fewer hands and the progressive elimination of the small capitalist on the one hand, and the ever closer and more elaborate organization of the proletariat on the other. At its climax the proletariat will arise, overthrow the capitalist class and expropriate them of the means of production, just as the capitalists displaced or absorbed the privileged hereditary classes with whom authority formerly resided.

In accordance with the theory that political events reflect preceding economic changes, the victory of the proletariat will be accompanied by an accompanying alteration of social structure and the abolition of the divisions between classes.

It would be difficult to overestimate the influence of this theory on working class thought; it has played a much larger part than Marx's Theory of Value in making his name venerated as the father of Socialism. The secret of its attraction lies in the fact that it gives the working classes the assurance of being on the winning side. The mere process of the unfolding of history in accordance with the unalterable principles of social evolution, whereby political changes follow and reflect economic changes, will, in due course, lead to the dispossession of the capitalist class. What then of the struggle, the class war, and the rising of the proletariat? Are these too inevitable? Does evolution proceed by violent and abrupt changes? Or can we not trust to the slow process of natural growth to bring about the social transformation we desire?

The different answers which have been given to these questions have given rise to the schools of evolutionary and revolutionary Socialism respectively. The first school, which has on the whole been predominant in Great Britain, emphasizes the biological aspect of Marx's work. Society, from the very fact that it is a product of and subject to evolution, is an organism, a living structure which, like any other living being, may grow or decay. Growth and decay are slow processes; they may be detected by human intelligence and even assisted and accelerated by human effort, but they cannot be reversed or brought to a standstill, nor can they be speeded up into abrupt and catastrophic changes.

The path of progress consists, therefore, in a series of reforms designed to assist the gradual movement of Society towards the next transformation, a transformation which will consist rather in the sum total of these reforms than in any abrupt change of structure consequent upon them. It is this school of evolutionary Socialism, known also as Collectivist or State Socialism, whose doctrines will form the subject of the remainder of this chapter.

There are, however, many Socialists who place a very different interpretation on Marx's theories. Whatever may be the position in the future, they emphasize the fact that Society, as it is to-day, is composed of two mutually opposed classes, the possessing and the dispossessed, who have no interests in common. Between them is a gulf which only a revolution involving a complete transformation of society can bridge. It may be true that Society will change and evolve in the natural course of events, but meanwhile the lives of the exploited workmen are passed in misery and suffering, and they cannot afford to wait. Every possible step must therefore be taken to hasten the next transformation of society, which is envisaged in terms of a complete change of economic and political structure, consequent upon a struggle in which the militant working classes resort to violence in order to achieve the expropriation of the capitalists.

This interpretation of Marx, which lies at the basis of Communism, and also in part of Syndicalism, will be followed out in a later chapter.

B. *The Reaction from Individualism.* Other forces were at work during the latter half of the nineteenth century, which helped to increase the dissatisfaction with capitalist society provoked by Marx's work. These forces sprang from a new conception of political theory, which tended to regard the State as a living organism, subject to growth and decay, and it is this conception which was adopted by the evolutionary Marxians. From 1870 onwards the creed of the Individualists had, as we have seen, come increasingly to be abandoned, and in *Fabian*

Essays, first published in 1889, the death knell of *laissez faire*, at any rate in its nineteenth-century form, was sounded.

The criticisms to which the doctrine of *laissez faire* is exposed have already been stated in our chapter on Individualism, and there is no need to restate them here. It was chiefly on its economic side that Individualism had broken down. There is no point in telling a man that he will always choose what is for his own interest when he has no choice but to sell his labour to the highest bidder; nor does it comfort a man who is starving in the gutter as an alternative to accepting a semi-starvation wage, that he enjoys the benefits of Freedom of Contract, and may pursue his own ends without fear of interference from the State. The miseries of long hours and low wages, of stunted lives and restricted development, which the Factory Acts and, later, the Trade Boards Acts were designed to mitigate, had shown how injurious were the unchecked operations of the law of supply and demand to the health and happiness of society. It became in fact increasingly evident that if the mass of the people were to rise above the level of mere wage slaves, they would have to be protected against the evils of free and unrestricted competition, by a greater measure of interference with and regulation of industry on the part of society than had been customary in the past.

The body politic is like the human body at least in this, that if any particular member is allowed to indulge its desires unchecked, the result reacts unfavourably upon the rest of the organism; and the freedom of a privileged class to pursue their private interests unchecked was prejudicing the welfare of the whole.

'In any society political organization is necessary because common action is necessary to repair the disorganization caused by the fact that men act independently and yet affect one another by such action.' [1]

[1] A. D. Lindsay, *The Theory of the State* (Bedford College Lectures, p. 104).

Economic action of the type that *laissez faire* encourages may be termed blind, in the sense that, though it proceeds from a number of individual wills, it has results which no one of the 'willing' individuals desires, and which extend far beyond the immediate circle of those who willed the action. A typical example of economic action is afforded by the behaviour of depositors when it is rumoured that a bank is about to fail. Each depositor rushes to withdraw his money, and the result of the actions which each individual has separately willed is the one result which nobody wants, namely, the failure of the bank.

To prevent these evil effects resulting from the blindness of unchecked economic action State action is necessary, and the first and most important aspect of the reaction from Individualism is, accordingly, the insistence on the necessity of State action to check the results of unrestricted profit-making.

The second is an increasing tendency to question the right of property-owners to the whole of the profits accruing from the joint efforts of masters and men. It is possible, while refusing to accept the whole of the Marxist doctrine on the subject of Exchange Value, not only to deny the right of the capitalist to all the profits which his ownership of the means of production obtains for him, but even to doubt the necessity for having capitalists at all. It is on these lines that the early propaganda of the Fabian Society proceeded.

The Fabians do not attack capital as the stolen funds of labour filched by the capitalist from the working man. On the contrary, they admit that on Marx's own premises the capitalist had a useful and even necessary part to play in the evolution of society. In initiating and managing, the capitalist was, at any rate in the early stages of the Industrial Revolution, undertaking an indispensable function in the organization of industry. He was, therefore, entitled to some part of the Exchange Value which his efforts conjointly with those of the workers created, even if he were never entitled to all of it and, as the control of industry becomes increasingly delegated to paid managers, is not now entitled to any.

But apart from the Exchange Value created mainly by the manual workers, of which Marx spoke, there are many values which are created wholly by the community, and these should be used, not for private profit, but for the benefit of the community which created them.

Thus the Fabians start by proposing that rent, that is to say, the 'unearned increment' of land, should be transferred from the landlord to society as a whole, seeing that it is society's need of the land which has made it valuable; and proposals of a similar kind are made in respect of all socially created values.

Instead of regarding the individual as an isolated unit who by his own unaided efforts makes his fortune, the Fabians insisted on the conception of society as a living body, whose needs and activities at all times co-operate with the individual in the creation of his wealth. Thus the extension of a town increases the value of land; so does the discovery of coal; so does the projection of a railway. Similarly, society's need of the great business pioneer takes the form of the payment of rent by society for his superior enterprise, initiative, and equipment. But the business man would be as helpless without society's need of his services as land would be valueless without society's need to build on it. In each case society has partially created the value, yet in each case society pays the rent.

This organic conception of society as the creator of value suggests the obvious conclusion, that what society creates it should control and enjoy. From this it is but a step to the assertion that the community as a whole should own the instruments of production, and that the community should own and administer the public services such as the railways, the mines, the roads, and the canals. The instruments of production and the public services would then be utilized for the benefit of all instead of being exploited for the enrichment of a few, and the community would then enjoy the value which it has itself created.

But it is clear that the community is not able in itself to undertake these manifold tasks : it must have some representative organ in which its will is expressed, which will work in accordance with its dictates and administer socially created values in its interests. This organ the Collectivist Socialist finds in the State.[1] A democratic State representative of the community as a whole and staffed by expert administrators who will utilize the resources of the community to the best advantage in the interests of the community, is thus the ideal in which Collectivist thought is embodied. The State must in fact be itself the workers. Only then will the workers it employs be working under their own dictates ; only then will those who own the means of production themselves be the users of those means.

It is worth while pausing at this point to see how far the reaction from Individualism has carried us. Instead of regarding the State as a clumsy nuisance whose interference with the beneficent working of private enterprise and free competition should be reduced to a minimum, we are now asked to think of it as the indispensable factor in social progress, through whose agency alone the worker is to be freed from the arbitrary conditions imposed upon him by the capitalist, and put in a position to enjoy the surplus value of which the privileged class has hitherto deprived him.

We are now in a position to describe both the philosophy which underlies Socialism, and the various measures which are proposed by Socialists with the object of giving this philosophy concrete expression.

[1] The 'State' here means the community organized collectively whether as Parish or District or Borough or County or Nation or (to include a Collectivist addition) as Consumers Co-operative Society.

II. *The Philosophy of Socialism.*

It is sometimes urged by Individualists that Socialism would have the effect of subordinating the individual to the State and so depriving him of his freedom. Although it is possible that some forms of Socialism might have that effect in practice, the intention of Socialism is exactly the reverse of this. Socialism in fact seeks to free the individual from the pressure of material cares, in order that he may live his life in his own way and freely develop his personality. But because the Socialist holds an organic view of the State as an entity composed of mutually dependent units, he believes that such freedom can only be achieved as the result of elaborate social organization.

The aims of the Socialist and the Individualist do not in the long run differ: each aims at giving to the individual the maximum amount of liberty. But while the Individualist thinks that this result can best be secured by the elimination of all outside checks and interferences in the relationship between man and man, the Socialist holds that it can only be achieved if men co-operate in Society to provide for each other the possibility of realizing a life which is at once full and free.

The Individualists spoke only of individuality, yet countenanced a system in which individuality was crushed by the pressure of material forces; the Socialists speak of work for society and the State, but they do so only in order that through society the individual may attain to a higher degree of self-development and personal freedom than he is able to realize in isolation. Socialism, in fact, carries the organization of society further than Individualism, not because it believes in efficiency for its own sake, but because it holds that a real individualism is only achieved when the individual is free to pursue spiritual ends.

The doctrine of Individualism received, as we have seen, a quasi-scientific sanction from the evolutionary theories of

Darwin. If existence is, from its very nature, a struggle, then free competition between man and man in which only the fittest survives is the only possible basis for society. Assuming, therefore, that human nature must be controlled by the struggle for life, the Individualist considered the aim of civilization to be the organization of that struggle in such a way that the greatest possible amount of life might survive. He thought, that is to say, in terms of quantity of life.

The Socialist, on the other hand, believes it to be possible to transcend the struggle for life, and regards civilization as that by means of which the struggle may be transcended. Life has some purpose other than the mere perpetuation of life ; quality of life is more important than quantity, and it is the business of civilization, by emancipating the individual from the exigencies of the bare struggle for existence, to put within his power the attainment of the highest *quality* of life.

The terms in which we shall envisage 'quality of life' will depend upon the kind of things we think valuable ; that is to say, upon our philosophy. Let us assume, however, that the good life consists, at any rate in part, in the ability to cultivate spiritual values, and to pursue spiritual ends which are good in themselves. The quest of truth for its own sake, the making of beautiful things because they are beautiful, the doing of right things because they are right, these, together with a certain level of physical and mental culture, an elevation of taste and a refinement of manners, are at least elements in the good life. Yet these things require leisure, knowledge, and a financial competence. They can only be achieved, that is to say, in so far as men are enabled to transcend the struggle for bare existence, and the secret of the Collectivist Socialist's veneration for the State lies in his belief that it is only by means of the State that this struggle can be transcended. As Mr. Clutton Brock puts it: 'The State exists not for its own power, which means the survival of its members or some of them, but so that its members may all be able to do those things which are worth doing.' 'Every State aims at a certain amount of co-operation, and is kept in being only because men are able to forget themselves in co-operation. The question is, therefore, the ultimate political question, why shall they co-operate? . . . No Socialist can be logically and thoroughly a Socialist unless he gives the right answer, which is that they shall co-operate so that they may, as far as possible, escape from the struggle of life to the doing of those things which are worth doing for their own sake.'

Hence the social creed which underlies the Socialist view of the State is that society is an association of human beings, formed with the object of giving all its members the opportunity to satisfy their desires for spiritual freedom and the good life.

Regarding society in this way, the Socialist not unnaturally expects men to work for it. Once the capitalist is expropriated and the workers are the State, men will feel that in working for society they are working for themselves; they will consent to regimentation by the State, because they know that the regulations they obey are inspired by a desire to further the common good; and they will do better work and do it more cheerfully, because of their knowledge that the fruits of their labour will go not to swell the profits of a private employer, but to enable men as a whole to live a fuller, a richer, and a freer life.

Socialism aims, then, at substituting the motive of social service for the motive of private profit. It holds that men will do better work to make the good life, with the leisure and financial competence it requires, possible for a society which in the long run is themselves, than they will at present consent to do for a society which compels them to enrich the exploiters of their labour in order to avoid starvation for themselves. If Socialism is wrong in making this assumption, if the psychology of human beings is such that they will not work willingly and well for society but only for themselves, then the whole of the Socialist edifice falls to the ground. For this doctrine is the foundation upon which it rests. Either men are socially minded in the sense described, or they are not, and cannot be made so. We shall, then, in our final chapter devote some consideration to this psychological assumption, since it is one which is equally involved by all forms of Socialist doctrine.

III. *Proposals and Policy of Collectivist Socialism.*

Socialism is defined in the *Encyclopaedia Britannica* (eleventh edition) as 'that policy or theory which aims at securing by the action of the central democratic authority a better distribution and, in due subordination thereto, a better production of wealth than now prevails'. This definition is not inappropriate to the aims and policy of Collectivist Socialism, and, with one very important exception, it adequately describes many if not most of the objects which all Socialists set before themselves. With the exception we shall deal later, contenting ourselves for the present with a description of the various measures which Socialists have proposed for securing (1) a better distribution of wealth, and (2) the regulation by society of the social life of the Community. The following are the most important, and they are those to which Socialists of any school would assent.

(1) The private ownership of the means of production to be abolished, and, with this object, important industries and services to be brought under public ownership and control.

(2) Industry to be carried on for the purpose of ministering to the needs of the community, and not with the object of making profits for individuals; the extent and character of production to be determined, therefore, not by anticipation of profit but by considerations of social need.

(3) The motive of social service, which is at present thwarted by the capitalization of industry, to be substituted for the incentive of private profit.

While the three propositions outlined above are matters of general agreement among Socialists, the various methods which are advocated with a view to their realization in practice are the subject of acute controversy. For the remainder of this chapter we shall be describing the policy of the Collectivist Socialists who belong to the evolutionary school. But it should be borne in mind that the schools of Socialism of which we shall give an account in our next two chapters would endorse very few of the various proposals, both as to means and ends, now to be described.

The methods which Collectivist Socialists propose to adopt, in order to accomplish the social transformation involved in the acceptance of the above three propositions, are strictly constitutional, and the agency through which they propose to effect the change is the existing State, the State being influenced by a gradual alteration in public opinion brought about by intensive Socialist propaganda and exercised through the ballot box. No sudden breach with the present system, involving a violent transition to a Socialist régime, is envisaged. True to the biological conception of society as a social organism, Collectivist Socialists have insisted that society is capable only of gradual change, and that each change must be conditioned by the nature of the social structure that preceded it. From this point of view it is essential to start with what exists and to allow the present to decide the direction, as well as the rapidity, of the steps which are taken into the future. The Fabians, who may be regarded as having set the pace for the Collectivist Socialists, have accordingly endeavoured quietly to permeate the Civil Service with their ideals, pressed for a policy of continual and unceasing State interference in and regulation of economic processes—a policy which has borne fruit in the Trade Boards Acts, the Health and Unemployment Insurance Acts, the Old Age Pension Acts, the extension of the powers of Local Government Authorities, and other measures of a Socialist tendency—and engaged in an extensive propaganda with the object of influencing public opinion on Socialist lines.

Not only do the Collectivist Socialists regard the State functioning by means of Parliamentary action as the instrument for effecting the desired series of gradual changes, but they look to it to undertake, when the transformation is complete, that regulation of social and economic life which they advocate. It is the machinery of Government which will effect the transition; and the machinery of Government, worked by a much strengthened Civil Service and considerably modified on democratic lines, will control administration when the transition is effected.

The question immediately arises, does Government mean the central Government, and is the State simply the Parliament at Westminster? Collectivists have resolutely disavowed such a conception, and in view of the criticisms which have been levelled against them on the ground of over-centralization, it is as well to emphasize the fact that Fabian Socialism, even in its earliest days, insisted on the importance of widening the scope and increasing the activity of Local Government.

Bernard Shaw, writing as early as 1889, declared that 'a democratic State cannot become a Social-democratic State unless it has in every centre of population a local governing body as thoroughly democratic in its constitution as the central Parliament', and in recent years, under the influence of criticism from Guild Socialists and other sources to which we shall refer in the next chapter, the current of Socialist thought in this country has turned increasingly in the direction of entrusting to the administration of Local Authorities many functions which were previously claimed for a centralized Civil Service. Thus we find the British Labour Party in their pamphlet, *Labour and the New Social Order*, which was published in 1919 and which constitutes in some ways the best modern statement of the immediate aims of evolutionary Socialists, pressing for the fullest possible scope in all branches of social reconstruction after the War to be given 'to the democratically elected local governing bodies'. While central Government Departments are to assist Local Authorities with information and grants in aid, and to insist on the maintenance of a certain minimum of efficiency, the latter are to be given 'a free hand to develop their own services over and above the prescribed minimum in whatever way they choose'. These services include, besides the control of water, gas, electricity, housing, and local transport, the provision of education, sanitation, and police, the planning of libraries and parks, the organization of public music and recreation, the retailing of coal, and the local distribution of milk. Matters in fact which affect not only the bodily health but the mental and spiritual well-being of men in their capacity of citizens are to be controlled and regulated by Local Authorities. It seems difficult then, at any rate so far as political administration is concerned, to endorse the charge of over-centralization which is commonly brought against Collectivism.

The measures advocated by the British Labour Party in the pamphlet referred to above are in general so instructive, and indicate so clearly the direction in which Collectivist Socialism is moving, the aims it sets before itself and the temper in which it pursues them, that it is proposed to enumerate the most important of them as typical expressions of moderate Socialist thought. They should be regarded both in the light of ends in themselves, and as means to an end beyond themselves; they are, that is to say, considered to be both desirable within the existing framework of society, and desirable in the sense that they will help to bring about a different and better state of society.

After stating their belief in the coming of a new social order based not on fighting but on fraternity, not on the competitive struggle for the means of bare life, but on a deliberately planned co-operation in production and distribution for the benefit of all who participate by hand or brain, the Labour Party make the following proposals :

(1) The Universal Enforcement of a National Minimum Wage;

(2) The Democratic Control of Industry;

(3) A Revolution in National Finance ; and

(4) The Employment of Surplus Wealth for the common good.

Proposal (1) is based on the affirmation of the State's obligation to ensure to every individual a wage which will provide all the requirements of a full development of mind, body, and character. With this object the Factory and Workshop Acts must be consolidated and extended, the working week reduced to not more than forty-eight hours, and the principle of equal pay for equal work recognized.

The duty of the State to prevent unemployment is also emphasized, and to further this object the raising of the school leaving age to sixteen is urged. When for any reason it proves impossible to find employment, arrangements must be made through the Trade Unions to provide full maintenance and training at public expense for those who are out of work.

Proposal (2) will be discussed more fully in the next chapter. For the present it may be noticed that it includes the usual Socialist provisions for the immediate nationalization of railways, mines, electricity, and canals ; urges the gradual elimination of the capitalist and the Joint Stock Company with appropriate compensation, and presses for the expropriation of the various profit-making Industrial Insurance Companies and the assumption by a State Department of the whole business of Life Assurance.

There are also recommendations as to education designed to secure that each member of the State, irrespective of his social class, shall be afforded an equal opportunity of developing his mental and spiritual powers and realizing all that he has it in him to be. Culture and knowledge must, it is urged, cease to be the privileged monopolies of a small class, and become the heritage of every citizen, a heritage to be freely enjoyed irrespective of the means of his parents.

The pamphlet then proceeds to problems of administration. The Labour Party are very much alive to the dangers of bureaucracy and over-centralization. There follow, therefore, the provisions for the enlarged activities and increased functions of Local Authorities at which we have already glanced, coupled with recommendations as to devolution in the shape of National Parliaments for Scotland, Wales, and England, co-ordinated by a central body at Westminster performing the functions of a Federal Assembly.

In the same strain we find detailed recommendations for the democratic control of industry by the workpeople engaged therein, which are coupled with the demand for national ownership. This section of the pamphlet is profoundly influenced by the developments in Socialist theory to be recorded in the next chapter.

Proposal (3) deals with the question of the source from which the money for the various schemes already detailed is to be obtained. Clearly no encroachment upon the national minimum standard of life must be permitted ; nor must the small incomes of the clerical and lower middle classes be threatened. The suggestion is accordingly made that the Income and Super Taxes should be radically revised and graduated in such a way as to make the real sacrifice of all the taxpayers approximately equal. This would involve a much steeper Income Tax graduation than exists at present, so that, while the lowest assessable class is paying a penny in the pound, the millionaire may be asked to pay as much as nineteen shillings.

This proposal is followed by a scheme for a Capital Levy, whereby the National War Debt is to be largely wiped out by a levy on the actual capital of all persons having an income exceeding, say, £1,000 a year.

These proposals indicate the implied assent of the Labour Party to the theory of Surplus Value, and their consequent determination to reduce private appropriation of Surplus Value almost to non-existence by transferring it indirectly, through the provision of State-aided schemes and grants, to those who have created it—a singularly British method of adapting and applying a somewhat doctrinaire theory.

(4) The fourth proposal is little more than a reaffirmation in general terms of the principle applied in the third. It describes as 'surplus' wealth the riches of the mines, the rental value of land above the margin of cultivation, and the material outcome of scientific discoveries; regrets that this surplus has hitherto been devoted to the luxury of an idle rich class, and proposes to impound it for the common good.

The Nationalization and Municipalization of important services will have the effect of taking much of this surplus out of private hands and transferring it into the public exchequer; and, where an industry remains temporarily under capitalist control, the steeply graduated income tax will divert to the State the great bulk of the profits. The mass of wealth thus acquired by the State is to be used for the provision of national education, for the maintenance of a high national minimum wage, for the care of the sick and infirm, for the endowment of maternity, for the encouragement of scientific research, and for the raising of the general standard of life of the community.

It will be seen that these latter proposals presuppose the existence of a Government permeated with Socialist ideals; they are, in fact, in the nature of ends rather than means, and of ends which can only be fully realized in a Socialist State.

The question naturally arises, 'What would such a State be like; what would be its structure, what its form of Government?' Mr. and Mrs. Sidney Webb have endeavoured to answer these questions in their book, *A Constitution for the Socialist*

Commonwealth of Great Britain. We refrain, however, from summarizing their proposals even in outline, partly owing to considerations of space, partly because they raise questions of a highly controversial character as to the relations between local and central Government, and the delimitation of the spheres of authority of the consumer and the producer respectively, both in politics and in industry, which fall more properly within the scope of the next chapter. Any one who wishes to acquaint himself with the type of Government advocated by exponents of the English school of moderate Socialism is recommended to read this profound and comprehensive work.

4

Syndicalism and Guild Socialism

Introductory.

WHEN quoting the definition of Socialism given in the eleventh edition of the *Encyclopaedia Britannica*, we took occasion to mention that with one important exception it adequately expressed the aims of the majority of Socialists to-day. It is with this exception that the present chapter will be concerned. It will be remembered that the definition in question spoke of Socialism as a doctrine 'which aims at securing by the action of *a central democratic authority*' a better distribution of wealth. If the phrase 'central democratic authority' means the existing State, many Socialists would now deny either that the central democratic authority is the agency through which a better distribution of wealth is to be effected, or that it provides the basis upon which the future Socialist society will be constructed.

The early years of the twentieth century witnessed a growing dissatisfaction with the State and with that body of political theory which, following Hegel, regards the State as an indispensable entity with mystically ideal attributes which must, in any society of however novel a type, necessarily exercise functions of sovereignty. In contradistinction to this view we get theories which regard the State as an association of consumers, one among many such associations to which the individual may belong, or as the machinery of government to be cheerfully scrapped and superseded by a different piece of machinery, should the latter prove more suited to the needs of the community, while the General Will is dismissed as a myth, or resolved into a number of different wills, each of which requires expression in a different type of representative body.

The experience of State control during the war has reinforced rather than removed the dissatisfaction with the State, and, as we have already seen, even Collectivist Socialism has been modified to a considerable extent by the prevalent hostility to centralized government.

Two schools of Socialists, the Syndicalists and the Guild Socialists, have taken the lead in the attack upon the Collectivist State.

Syndicalism, which is the earlier doctrine of the two, weights the balance against the State as markedly as the Collectivists had inclined it in its favour. Although, therefore, we shall consider it first in our survey, it need not detain us long, since most of what is valuable in the doctrine of the Syndicalists has been absorbed by the Guild Socialists, whose theory is the most coherent and carefully thought out of all the recent developments in Socialist doctrine.

I. *Syndicalism.*

Syndicalism is the name given both to a body of social doctrine or theory of social organization, and to a plan of action. The plan of action is a particular phase of what Marx called the class war, and its object is to bring into being a Syndicalist organization of society. While, however, the Syndicalist plan of action is direct, vigorous, and well defined, the state of society which it seeks to realize is extremely nebulous. The general outlines are indicated, though even these are hazy, but the details are wanting. There is a reason for this vagueness, a vagueness which is often deliberate, as we shall see when we come to consider the peculiar philosophy which is alleged to have influenced the Syndicalist leaders.

We shall describe first the Syndicalist theory of social organization, secondly the plan of action which Syndicalists advocate, and thirdly the philosophy which is said to underlie Syndicalism.

A. *Syndicalist Theory of Society.* Syndicalism may be defined as that form of social theory which regards the Trade Union organizations as at once the foundation of the new society and the instrument whereby it is to be brought into being. It is frankly socialistic in the sense that it adopts the general Socialist view of capital as theft, endorses or rather extends the notion of the class war as fundamental in capitalist society, and proposes to abolish the private ownership of the means of production and to substitute ownership by the community.

As opposed, however, both to Collectivist Socialism and to Communism, Syndicalism draws its inspiration from the work of Proudhon rather than from that of Marx. Proudhon's theory of Associative Communism envisaged a society which is in many respects very similar to the free organization of voluntary associations advocated by the Anarchists (see chapter 5, pp. 107–11). French Trade Unionism has been strongly influenced by the teaching of Proudhon, and has consequently developed from the first a marked 'localist' and anti-authoritarian tendency. This tendency has shown itself more particularly in the disposition to regard the Trade Union unit as the type of the voluntary association which is to succeed the capitalist State, and Syndicalism, which is the peculiar emanation of French Trade

Unionism, has never lost the Anarchist sympathies which it has derived from its origin.

The chief difference between Syndicalism and Collectivist Socialism lies in the insistence of the former on the importance of what is called producers' control. The workers who create value should, in the Syndicalist view, be the controllers of society; that is to say, Syndicalists hold that the workers as producers should exercise control not only in the economic or industrial sphere, but also in the political sphere, or, to put it more accurately, that the political sphere with its organ the State should cease to exist as such, and that its functions should be taken over by bodies of producers organized on a vocational basis. In this Syndicalism differs from Guild Socialism, since the latter, while sharing the Syndicalist objection to the interference of the State in the industrial sphere, which equally with Syndicalism it would hand over entirely to the producers, recognizes a need for further representation of the Common Will in the political sphere. In this respect, therefore, Guild Socialism occupies a middle position between Collectivism on the one hand and Syndicalism on the other.

It will be seen from the above that Syndicalism, in reaction from the State Socialism which tends to regard society as an organization of consumers only, goes to the other extreme in its insistence on the importance of the producer. Thus we find Pelloutier, one of the Syndicalist leaders, affirming that 'the task of the revolution is to free mankind not only from all authority but also from every institution which has not for its essential purpose the development of production'.

The objections of the Syndicalists to the State, and consequently to any form of State organization of society, may be briefly stated as follows.

In the first place there is a generalized though somewhat vague feeling of hostility to the State as a bourgeois and middle-class institution. The State is not only the instrument of capitalist exploitation in society as it is to-day, but, from its very nature, it would and must remain middle-class in the society of to-morrow. The service of the State makes men bureaucratic and unsympathetic to the needs and aspirations of those who are engaged in the actual work of production, and it would continue to have this effect under any system of society that retained the State. A central organization tends to uniformity, to routine, to lack of imagination and initiative, and to distrust of local development and enterprise. Even a benevolent State, therefore, would, if left in control of industry, be inimical to progress. But if the State has this effect on industry, it will have it in other directions. It is not the middle-class Civil Servant, but the manual worker, who knows what the manual worker wants, and it is to the manual worker, therefore, in his industrial organization, that it should fall to prescribe accordingly.

Allied to this dislike of the middle-class State is a distrust of middle-class Socialism. Syndicalism claims to be the only school of Socialist doctrine which is the product of the workers themselves; all other forms of Socialism have emanated from the brains of clever middle-class theorists, and betray their origin. They show a tendency to regiment the workers in conformity with some pre-arranged system of society which has seemed good to a clique of intellectuals. They are accordingly out of touch with the needs of the workers, which can only be adequately expressed by a system devised by the workers themselves. The importance of keeping alive an intense class consciousness further forbids any *rapprochement* between the workers and the intellectuals of the middle-class, even when the latter are favourably disposed, as inimical to revolutionary ardour.

In favour of a system of producers' control, it is argued that it will lead to an increase both of freedom for the workers and of efficiency in the industry. Where industry is owned and controlled by the Trade Unions, each worker participating therein has a direct voice in its management. He therefore enjoys the substance of democracy in every act of his working life, as compared with the misleading shadow which is offered to him once every few years under a political system, when he is invited to cast a vote into the ballot-box to enable the least unsuitable of three or four unsuitable candidates, none of whom he has selected for himself, to misrepresent him in a national Parliament. Having a personal interest in the conduct of industry he will take a pride in his work, and the quantity and quality of his output will both be improved.

Although, as we have already noticed, we are never told in detail what form society as a whole would assume under a Syndicalist régime, there are various indications of the way in which the economic and industrial side of the nation's life would be organized. It should be noted, however, that the details of the different schemes proposed vary with and reflect the structure of the particular movement from which the scheme emanates. The doctrines which are most typical of Syndicalist thought are of French origin; and in order to put the reader in a better position to understand the organization of society proposed for the future, it will be desirable to devote a few paragraphs to a description of the French Trade Union organization of to-day.

The body which has taken the chief part in popularizing Syndicalism is the French Confédération Générale du Travail. This Confederation is composed of two different kinds of bodies. In the first instance it comprised some seven hundred Syndicats, that is to say, Trade Unions of workmen engaged in the same industry or in the same process of industry. These Syndicats were legalized in 1884 and were first federated into the C. G. T. in 1895. Parallel but somewhat different organizations of French working men had grown up simultaneously with the Syndicats. These were the Bourses du Travail. A Bourse du Travail comprised workmen belonging to many different trades, who happened to live in the same locality. Its functions were to serve as a local Labour Exchange for its members and generally to champion the rights of labour in its locality. In 1893 the Bourses were brought together in a Fédération des Bourses du Travail. This Federation coalesced in 1902 with the C. G. T., with the result that an organization was formed in which each local Syndicat figured twice over, once together with the other Syndicats of workers in the same trade as representing the needs and interests of that particular trade, and once, together with the other Syndicats of workers in the same locality, in the local Bourse du Travail, as representing the needs and interests of that particular locality. This organization was largely the work of Pelloutier, quoted above, and the adoption by it of a Syndicalist policy was mainly due to his influence.

Now the organization of society envisaged by the French Syndicalist after the Revolution is clearly modelled upon that of the C. G. T. The local Syndicats, which will of course be all inclusive, will be federated into a Bourse which will act both as an employment agency for the district and as a centre of Trade Union activities. The Bourse will be in touch with the economic needs of the locality, and will co-operate, therefore, with other neighbouring Bourses with a view to the provision of those needs. It will, that is to say, both determine the nature and extent of production in the industries in its locality, and, in co-operation with the Bourses of other districts, the importation and exportation of products from and to these districts.

This extremely local system of organization, which reflects the parochialism of French industrialism, is nevertheless typical of Syndicalism wherever it appears. As we have already mentioned, Syndicalism is strongly influenced by the theories of Proudhon, and the adoption of the Bourse as the basis of social organization is no doubt suggested by his system of local units. It would, of course, prove quite unsuitable in countries such as Great Britain, where industry is organized on a larger scale, and it was probably a recognition of this fact, and also of the need for making some provision for the consumers' point of view (a need emphasized by the Guild Socialists, whose theories have exercised a considerable influence on later developments of Syndicalism), which led the Syndicalist Congress at Lyons in 1919 to demand the 'industrialized *nationalization* of the great services of modern economy: land and water transport, mines, water power, and credit organizations', and to define *nationalization* as the confiding of national property to the interested parties, namely, the associated producers and *consumers*.

Despite these later developments the tendency to base the organization of society upon the smallest industrial unit is characteristic of most Syndicalist doctrine in its typical form; it appears in the declarations of the Industrial Workers of the World, an American Syndicalist body, and is a tenet which indicates the common origin of Syndicalism and Anarchism.

B. *Methods of Syndicalism.* As might have been expected from the bias against the State already described, Syndicalists are distrustful of political methods as a means of achieving the changes in society which they desire. The experience of witnessing among working-class leaders newly elected to the national Parliament a gradual loss of revolutionary ardour, followed by the adoption of a bourgeois policy of constitutional melioration, has been particularly frequent in France, and has resulted in the conviction that the workers must rely solely upon themselves. The Labour M.P. represents not his Trade Union but his constituents, and for this very reason cannot, even if he would, devote himself to the workers' cause. The worker must accordingly be prepared to obtain authority in the State not mediately through M.P.s or delegates, but immediately through the strength of his Union. Hence the Syndicalist has stood everywhere for a policy of 'direct action' in the economic sphere, which he is prepared, if necessary, to interpret as violent action.

Thus Syndicalism starts with the general presumption that economic power is the key to the position. This view, which is held as a matter of principle for which good authority is found in Marx, is reinforced by considerations of strategy. Workmen hold different political opinions, but they have the same economic interests; they are imbued, therefore, with a sense of solidarity in the industrial sphere which is wanting in the political; they will strike together when they will not vote together. In any event a political party is a poor revolutionary weapon; it is dispersed, it meets rarely, and it is apt to be too large to afford a direct expression of the common will.

For a variety of reasons, then, the Syndicalist is led to concentrate on the economic sphere, and in that sphere his chief weapon is the strike. Strikes are encouraged whenever and wherever possible; strikes for better wages, strikes for shorter hours, and above all strikes for more control. Such strikes are both good in themselves and good as a means to something beyond themselves. They are good in themselves because, even when they fail, they give the workers a sense of solidarity, a lesson in self-discipline, and a feeling of self-reliance, while serving at the same time to intensify the class war, and to throw into clear relief the alignment of the nation into two hostile parties, the dispossessed proletariat on the one hand and the possessing capitalist class on the other. They are good as a means because they tend to bring nearer the day of the general strike.

The doctrine of the general strike as the weapon which will ultimately bring the revolution to pass is in part derived from the French Socialist writer, Blanqui. The general strike is not necessarily a strike of all workers. On the contrary, it is not to be expected that an adequate number of the workers will be animated by a sufficiently vigorous class-conscious spirit to strike simply and solely for the purpose of terminating the capitalist system. What is wanted is a strike on the part of a sufficient proportion of the workers in key industries to secure the paralysis of capitalism. In this respect the growing complexity and interdependence of modern industry will make the general strike at once easier and more effective, by rendering it possible for a minority of the workers to paralyse the whole of industry. As soon as a class-conscious minority of the workers of sufficient numerical strength can be brought to the requisite fighting pitch, a general strike will be declared and the instruments of production seized. This will be the end of capitalism.

The circumstance that a general strike of this character will be undemocratic in the sense that it may well be opposed to the wishes of the majority of the workers, is of no importance. The dogma of majority rule is dismissed as a mere bourgeois superstition, and it is realized that, at any rate during the transitional stage, it will be necessary for a minority to seize the reins of power and guide the rest of the workers towards their own salvation.

In this respect the Syndicalists depart from the strict letter of Marx's teaching, or at any rate place a new interpretation upon it. In prophesying that capitalist society in the process of its evolution would in due course reach a stage at which the proletariat would rise and dispossess their masters, they hold that Marx was unduly optimistic. The employers will not be so ready to fight for their class as Marx supposed; they will bargain and compromise and obscure in a thousand ways the distinction between workers and masters, until the revolutionary edge is taken off the workers' spirit. In these circumstances the workers must adopt and carry out by all means in their power a policy of perpetual offence. Although the strike is their strongest weapon, there are also various forms of sabotage—from doing bad work, breaking machinery, and spoiling work which has already been done, to obeying the letter of all rules exactly and literally in such a way as to prevent industry from being carried on. There is the policy of the boycott and the label which shows that work has been done under Trade Union conditions, and there is 'ca' canny', or the practice of doing a minute quantity of work with scrupulous care.

All these methods may be practised (although certain forms of sabotage and 'ca' canny' are objected to by some of the Syndicalist leaders as destructive of morale) both for their educative effect and because they tend to make easier the way of the general strike.

C. *Philosophy of Sorel.* It will doubtless be thought that the general strike is envisaged in very vague terms; but the vagueness is deliberate, as deliberate as the Syndicalist refusal to paint any very definite picture of the state of society that will succeed it. This vagueness and this refusal are perhaps due in part to the influence of the French writer Sorel. The work of Sorel is a queer combination of politics and philosophy, a strange application of a popular metaphysical theory to social problems. What in fact Sorel has done is to invoke Bergson's theory of Intuition, which the average Syndicalist would be the last to understand, to justify a course of action of which Bergson would be the first to disapprove.

The philosopher Bergson, whose system became very popular in France during the last decade of the nineteenth century and the first of the twentieth, held that the ends of our actions are not set for us by reason but by Intuition. Our intellect tells us how we may do what we want to do, but it plays no part whatever in determining what we do want to do. Not only, however, does Intuition determine the ends at which we aim, but it is Intuition which grasps the nature and meaning of the Universe in so far as we can comprehend them at all. But the vision that Intuition gives us, although perfectly clear, is nevertheless not one that can be explained in concrete, rational terms to one who does not share it. It is a purely private and personal thing, irrational like an act of faith, yet compelling to action on the part of all those who have it, like a religious belief.[1]

Now it is this theory of Intuition, a theory primarily designed to describe our apprehension of metaphysical truth, that Sorel uses in justification of a General Strike which is unable to give a rational account of its objects. The workers are not, in Sorel's view, to be told in any detail what the General Strike is for, nor what kind of society it is to introduce. Their apprehension of the state of society which is the goal of all their activities is in fact to be intuitional; that is to say, it is neither to be communicated by rational teaching nor to take shape as a rational conviction. In Sorel's language the general strike is to be a 'myth' to the workers, a myth being an idea which fills men with ardour, as the expectation of Christ's second coming inspired the early Christians. But any attempt to rationalize the myth is bound to be misleading. For the purpose of estimating the worth or purpose of the general strike, 'all the methods of discussion which are current among politicians, sociologists, or people who pretend to political science, must be abandoned'.

One of the merits of this doctrine is that, by enabling Sorel to convict of irrelevance not only criticism but even discussion of the general strike, it makes the conception unassailable. It would be difficult to find a better weapon for the purposes of political controversy. What is true of the general strike is true in a lesser degree of any strike. Because strikes are undertaken from motives which lie deep down in the intuitional part of our natures, 'they'—that is to say, sporadic strikes—'have engendered in the proletariat the noblest, deepest, and most moving senti-

[1] For a fuller account of Bergson's Theory of Intuition, see chapter on Bergson in the *Introduction to Modern Philosophy*, World's Manuals Series, by the same author.

ments they possess; the general strike groups them all in a co-ordinated picture, and by bringing them together, gives to each one of them its maximum intensity. . . . We thus obtain that intuition of socialism which language cannot give us with perfect clearness—and we obtain it as a whole, perceived instantaneously.'

It is important that we should not overestimate the effect of this teaching on the Syndicalist movement—important, if for no other reason, because many writers have in fact overestimated it. The average workman is not a Bergsonian, nor has he ever heard of 'Intuition'. Even among the leaders it is doubtful if Sorel has had much influence. The Syndicalist movement came first, and Sorel, an unsolicited apologist, came after. In some respects, too, Syndicalism has developed a bias contradictory to Sorel's teaching. For instance, Sorel and the theorists detest sabotage: loitering at a task suggests to them that the workman is not fitted for revolution. At the same time, however, it would be idle to deny that Sorel's teaching does give a quasi-rational justification to what must otherwise seem a policy of mere impatience, the advocacy of a general 'blowing up' for its own sake, and it is a justification that accords well with the impatient temper of Syndicalist propaganda. What is of importance in Sorel's view is his contention that, beyond the actual strike, nothing is thought out, and nothing need be thought out. Sorel has tried to show that a policy of destruction is not necessarily a policy of despair, and Syndicalism has not failed to grasp at so convenient a theory. Syndicalist propaganda was very prominent both in France and the United States in the years immediately preceding the war. It should be remembered, however, (1) that it has made comparatively little headway since the war, (2) that it has never had much following in this country. It is too doctrinaire, too extreme, and too logical to be popular among a race of natural compromisers; and the school of thought known as Guild Socialism, which has drawn equally upon State Socialism and upon Syndicalism for its beliefs, has won far more converts in this country than Syndicalism has done, or is ever likely to do. It is this theory of Socialism which we must now consider.

II *Guild Socialism.*

It will be convenient to divide our treatment of Guild Socialism into three parts. We shall first glance at its antecedents, then describe the general principles upon which it is based and the objects at which it aims, and conclude by a brief survey of the methods which it advocates for the purpose of achieving those objects.

A. *Antecedents of Guild Socialism.* The history of Guild Socialism need not detain us long. It is in origin a purely English theory, which may be said to have first attracted attention with the publication in 1906 of a book by A. J. Penty, entitled *The Restoration of the Guild System.* In this book Mr. Penty advocates a return to the medieval principle of self-government in industry, whereby the craftsman who was a member of an autonomous Guild owned the instruments with which he worked, and determined the nature and extent of his production. Mr. Penty's argument is based partly on sentimental, partly on aesthetic grounds, and is animated throughout by a hostility to modern methods of production and trading on a large scale. For this reason the proposals made for organizing industry on the basis of the independent craftsman are not practical politics to-day, and it may be doubted whether they were ever intended as such. The work of Penty represents the Utopian phase of Guild Socialist propaganda, just as that of William Morris represents the Utopian stage of Socialism proper.

It was not until 1909 that the theory assumed a more practical form. The years 1909–12 were years of great labour unrest, in which the Trade Unions played an increasingly important part. The proposal was accordingly put forward by writers such as

S. G. Hobson and A. R. Orage in the columns of the *New Age*, that the Guild idea should be adapted to modern conditions on the basis of the existing Trade Union organization. Their plea was for self-government in industry by the workers concerned in the industry, grouped together in a system of industrial Guilds, of which the existing Trade Unions would form the germ. By 1912 the Guild idea had become for the first time a definite force in the British Labour movement, and its influence may thenceforward be seen in all the more important statements of aims and demands issued by the various organizations which form the movement. This is notably the case in the miners' scheme for the nationalization and management of the mines, which was laid before the Coal Industry Commission in 1919, and which comprises many of the leading features of Guild Socialist theory. Early in 1915 the National Guilds League was founded, with the object of initiating propaganda in favour of the Guild idea throughout the Labour movement; and although the mass of the workers has remained comparatively unaffected by this propaganda, many of the leaders of Labour, especially among the younger men, are to-day in a greater or less degree converts to Guild Socialism.

The Guild Socialists, then, may best be described as a small body of intellectual theorists working within the Labour movement with the object of converting the influential men of the movement to their views, but not as a general rule making any direct appeal for the support of the masses.

B. *Principles and Objects of Guild Socialism.* The goal at which the National Guilds League aims is described as the 'abolition of the Wage-System, and the establishment by the workers of Self-Government in industry, through a democratic system of National Guilds, working in conjunction with other democratic functional organizations in the community'. The general principles on which this statement of aims is founded may be reduced to three, of which the second and the third are particular applications of the first.

These are: (1) the principle of Functional Democracy; (2) the principle that industry should be administered by the common action of workers both of hand and brain who carry on the industry; and (3) the principle that power and responsibility in society should be related and proportional to the importance of the functions which individuals perform in the service of the community.

(1) The principle of Functional Democracy is of considerable interest for Political Theory, and it is worth while to examine it in some detail. It has been elaborated and applied to the solution of questions both of industrial and of political organization by G. D. H. Cole, who has written extensively on Guild Socialist theory. The application of the theory in the political and administrative spheres is not, however, accepted by all Guild Socialists who adopt it in the industrial. It may be stated as follows. It is impossible for any one person to represent any other person; hence all so-called representative institutions that have existed in the past are misrepresentative institutions. But although a man cannot represent his neighbours, he can represent a group of purposes which his neighbours have in common. Thus X can represent the common interests of A, B, and C, who are all football players, as football players; Y can represent the common interests of A, D, and E, who are all builders, as builders; and Z can represent the interests of A, F, and G, who are all Presbyterians, as Presbyterians; but neither X nor Y nor Z, whether taken separately or together, can be said adequately to represent all the interests of A, or in other words A himself. It follows that any kind of representation which really represents must be functional representation, and that the only bodies which are really democratic, in the sense that they express the will of those who elect them, are those which are related to the various func-

tions which individuals perform. A democratic society will, therefore, be one which is a co-ordinated network of functional representative bodies, each of which represents a particular set of wills or purposes which its members have in common.

Let us see of what kind of bodies a functional democracy constructed on these lines would consist. In the first place there are the various interests which men have in common because they are members of the same country, the political interests with which Political Theory has hitherto been almost exclusively concerned. These are taxation and law, defence against foreign aggression, and the maintenance of a certain standard of education. These are national affairs affecting equally all the dwellers in a particular geographical area, and men's wills in respect of them are best represented on a national body not dissimilar to the existing Parliament. Then there is the provision of gas and water, of a police force to maintain order, of local amenities, of a minimum standard of sanitation and so forth; these are matters in which men are interested because they dwell in the same local area. A local Regional body after the model of the existing Local Authority is, therefore, the appropriate organ for the expression of the individual's will in such matters.

Then there is production; this gives rise to a set of special problems peculiar to itself in respect of which a new form of representation is required. Questions of status, of conditions, of hours, wages, and amount of output can only be adequately settled in accordance with the common will as expressed on workshop and factory committees elected for the purpose. But the nature and extent of production, and the prices of the articles produced, are matters which also touch the consumer. Consumers' Councils are, therefore, required to consult with the bodies of producers. The function of these Councils will be to determine, in conjunction with the workshop and factory committees of producers, questions of costs and prices. Religion again is a separate sphere, and the expression of the individual's will within it is distinct from the other interests we have touched.

Thus the theory of functional democracy, reacting vigorously from the idea of a centralized and all-embracing State, advocates devolution of powers and functions to a number of different bodies, which will, it is hoped, adequately express all the varied interests of man in the complex of modern society.

Now it is something of an historical accident that this particular theory of democracy, which, if it is valid, is valid throughout the whole body politic, should have been first applied to industry. It was so applied by the Guild Socialists for two reasons. In the first place they adopted Marx's view that 'economic power precedes political power'. They held, that is to say, that no democracy was possible in the political sphere unless there was first democracy in the economic sphere, and that, if industry were organized democratically, the democratic organization of society would necessarily follow. The second reason was that modern industry is in such a chaotic condition that, until it is re-established on an orderly basis, there can be no health in any other department of social life. The Guild Socialist urges, that is to say, that the methods and motives of Capitalism are demonstrably breaking down in industry, and that some substitute for Capitalism will have sooner or later to be found, if only for the reason that the workers are failing to maintain the level of production under the existing system.

The fact, therefore, that the Guild Socialist applies his theory of functional democracy to the industrial sphere does not mean that it is inapplicable in the political and social spheres. He contends, on the contrary, that the principle of functional democracy should be extended to local and national Government, and proposes accordingly so to extend it after it has been applied in industry.

(2) and (3). As applied to industry the principle takes the

following form. The chief public services and industries are to be owned by the State (so far the Guild Socialist is in agreement with the Collectivist). But, though nationalization is desirable, it must not be assumed that industrial problems will be solved by the mere transference of industry to public ownership.

Guild Socialists make much of the evils of bureaucracy. They point to the fact that the employees of public bodies such as the London County Council, or even of the great State Departments, are not noticeably better off in the matter of wages and conditions than the workers in privately owned concerns, and demonstrate conclusively that an expert Civil Service, even if it were capable of conducting a publicly owned industry efficiently, would be out of touch with the needs of the workers, and unamenable to suggestions from below. In order, then, that industry may be really democratic it must be organized from below. Foremen and managers must be elected by and held responsible to the workers themselves, so that control of the administration of industry may be effectively exercised by the organized workers in the industry. Such control is to be vested in a Guild.

The Guild is modelled on the existing Trade Union, but differs from it in two important respects. In the first place it would include all the workers both by hand and brain, from the errand boy to the manager, who are concerned in a particular industry. In the second place its chief function would be not to protect the interests of its members but to carry on the industry.

From the above differences in aims and constitution it follows that the actual practice of the Guilds would differ from the practice of the Trade Unions in two ways.

(*a*) Owing to the fact that it falls to the Trade Union to protect its members against capitalist aggression, it has historically been concerned almost exclusively with the attempt to raise wages and shorten hours.

(*b*) Any attempt on the part of the Trade Unions to take a share in control, while the control is still in the hands of the employer, must necessarily be of a negative character. It takes the form of saying: 'This shall not be done,' or 'This shall not be done in this way,' rather than 'This shall be done,' or 'This shall be done in this way'. Hence arises a mistaken notion that the Trade Unions are from their very nature obstructive and hostile to industrial efficiency.

But it is clear that these differences in practice arise from the fact that the Trade Union is organized for militant purposes in a hostile society, while the Guild will be organized for peaceful purposes in a friendly society. A Trade Union which is organized for peace and production and not for warfare and self-protection, which is really inclusive of all the workers in the industry and in complete control of all matters affecting production—a Trade Union, that is to say, which *is* a Guild—will, from the very fact that it is working directly for the community, and that in doing so it is representing the common will of the workers as producers, be able not only to maintain production at the capitalist level but to increase and improve it. And it will do this because it will draw upon the motive of social service which is baulked and stifled in industry as organized at present.

It is to this fact, namely, that the Guilds will be working in the service of the community, that Guild Socialists look, at any rate in part, for their answer to the obvious charge that there is nothing to prevent a Guild, which has a monopoly of production in the particular industry for which it stands, exploiting the public in its own interests. Whether they are right in doing so only the event can prove. It may be that the motive of social service which admittedly exists would not prove strong enough in practice to overcome the incentive to private gain; it may be that men are private spirited always and in all things before they are public spirited. If this be the case, then Guild Socialism would break down, resolving itself into an anarchy of exploiting

Guilds whose opportunities of fleecing the community would exceed those of the capitalist employer in proportion as they would have a more complete monopoly of production. But the breakdown of Guild Socialism on this question of psychology would mean the breakdown of any other form of Socialism ; for if men cannot be persuaded sometimes to put the good of the community first and their own good (except in so far as they benefit when the community benefits) second, then the only possible basis for society is the present basis of profit-making and competition. As we have already remarked, this is the ultimate psychological question on the answer to which our attitude to any form of Socialist doctrine will depend, and it is proposed briefly to discuss it in a separate chapter.

It should, however, be pointed out that, though Guild Socialists admit that in the long run the workability of their scheme depends upon a certain conception of human nature, they have nevertheless provided a system of checks against any tendency on the part of the Guilds to overcharge the community for the goods they produce.

In the first place the plea of the Guild Socialists for producers' control is advanced only with regard to the actual running of the industry. They believe that industry should be run on the one hand by technical experts who understand its scientific and commercial side, and on the other by the manual workers who are actually engaged in turning out the goods. But this is not a demand for the entire control of the economic process from the beginning of production to the end of consumption. It is a demand which is confined to those processes involved in the actual turning out and distribution of the goods. So soon as questions of prices and division of surplus products arise, then the consumers' interests become involved, and, in accordance with the theory of functional democracy, the consumers' will with regard to these questions must be expressed in Consumers' Councils, which, acting in co-operation with the Producers' Guilds, will fix prices and determine the distribution of surplus goods.

Mr. Cole recognizes three different kinds of bodies of consumers which should, he thinks, co-operate with three different types of Guild in settling questions of this kind. In the first place there are the great national industries and services, the mines, the railways, coal, shipping, and so forth. These will be owned by the State, which will appoint *ad hoc* national bodies representing the point of view of the public, to consult with the big national Guilds in which the workers in these industries will be organized. In the second place there are the Public Utility Services, gas, water, electricity, local transport, and so forth. These will pass into municipal rather than national ownership, and the local consumers, represented in bodies not dissimilar to Local Authorities, will negotiate in such matters with the local Guilds responsible for the conduct of these services in the districts concerned. In the third place there is a mass of small-scale industries engaged in the production of commodities which are consumed individually in the home. The retail distribution of goods at present carried out by small privately owned shops may be regarded as an industry which also belongs to this class. These industries, in Mr. Cole's view, will not at any time pass through a stage either of nationalization or of municipalization. He suggests that the Co-operative Movement will assume their ownership, and that bodies of Co-operators elected both on a regional and on a national basis will be the appropriate Consumers' Councils to negotiate with the Guilds engaged in organizing the workers in these industries, with regard to fixing prices and arranging matters of distribution.

By these and similar means the Guild Socialist seeks to give the consumer, represented in various types of Consumers' Councils, a sufficient safeguard against exploitation on the part of the workers who are engaged in controlling production and organizing the conditions under which production takes place. Taxation will constitute an additional means of removing the temptation on the part of the Guild to amass excessive profits at the expense of the community. A steeply graded tax imposed upon industries at the source and payable by the Guilds would redress any inequality in the matter of profits between the Guilds.

The question arises as to the position and functions of the State under such a scheme. We have spoken of the nationalization of certain industries and referred to certain matters, such as national defence, the maintenance of law and order, and the assessment of taxation, as being the concern of national bodies representative of all citizens dwelling within the national boundaries. But little has been said up to the present of the nature of these bodies, and their relationship to the national Parliament as at present constituted. On this point there is some difference of opinion among Guild Socialists. Many refuse to lay down in advance any hard and fast rules as to the political structure which a Guild Socialist society would assume. Thus the National Guilds League holds 'that the exact form of organization in any country cannot be determined in advance of the situation which calls it into being'. In general, however, the League adopts a hostile attitude to the State and follows Marx's teaching in regarding it, as at present organized, as 'an Executive Committee for administering the affairs of the whole capitalist class'. This hostility to the State regarded as a repository of sovereignty in the community continues after the transformation of society into a Guild Socialist community has been achieved. There is a tendency to relegate the State to the role of an association of consumers, represented on a number of bodies elected on a national basis for the purpose of negotiating with the big producing Guilds.

Others, however, take the view that there will remain, under a Guild Socialist régime, certain functions which only a body resembling the State as it exists to-day on its political side can fulfil, and in the light of the considerations mentioned in our third chapter (see pp. 46–48) there seems to be little doubt that they are right.

C. *Methods of Guild Socialists.* We must in conclusion glance briefly at the methods which Guild Socialists advocate with the object of bringing a Guild Socialist society into being.

Guild Socialists pride themselves on the intensely practical character of the form of Socialism which they advocate. Although it is fully realized that no transition to a state of Socialism is likely in practice to be effected without some measure of violence, there is, nevertheless, no theoretical reason why a Guild Socialist state should not be established as a result of purely evolutionary processes. In building, as it does, upon the existing organization of the Trade Unions, Guild Socialism endeavours to throw a bridge across the gulf which separates a Capitalist from a Socialist society. The Trade Unions are the key to the situation in two ways. In the first place the Trade Unions of to-day will become the Guilds of to-morrow ; in the second place the Trade Unions are the organizations by means of which the actual transition is to be accomplished.

As we have remarked above, there is no essential difference, so far as structure is concerned, between the Trade Union and the Guild, although in two important respects the Trade Unions will have to be modified before they can fulfil the functions of the Guild. They must be made all inclusive of the workers in the industry, and they must assume some measure of control in the working of the industry. Guild Socialist propaganda is, therefore, largely directed to securing these two essential modifications in Trade Union structure and functions. In the first place it advocates larger and fewer Trade Unions, and endeavours to remodel Trade Union structure along the lines of vertical as opposed to horizontal organization. A vertical organization would embrace all the workers in a particular industry from top to bottom, including both the manager and the errand boy. A horizontal organization would include workers performing one particular process or set of processes, which may happen to be the same in a number of different industries. It is clear that such horizontal or craft Unions, as they are called, of which there are many to-day, will possess a narrower and more sectional outlook than that of the large industrial Unions.

In the second place there is, or there was until the last few years, an increasing disposition on the part of Trade Unions, as a result of Guild Socialist propaganda, to interfere in questions of discipline and management within the factory. The more militant Trade Unions have pursued a policy which is called the policy of 'encroaching control', of which the object is to transfer to the workers as many as possible of the functions of control without actually dispossessing the capitalist. This policy has two outstanding features. The first is a claim on the part of the Trade Unions that the foremen and overseers in a factory should be elected by the rank and file workers organized in the Trade Unions, together with the corresponding claim that foremen to whom the workers object should be dismissed. The organization of industry from below is, as we have seen, one of the fundamental principles of Guild Socialist theory, and although the number of cases in which the Trade Unions have been able to secure the election of foremen by their members has been small, the concession of the right in one or two cases has, nevertheless, been regarded as an important step in the direction of workers' control.

The second important feature of the policy of 'encroaching control' is the 'Collective Contract'. In one or two cases a Trade Union was able during the war to conclude with an employer or set of employers a single collective agreement determining not only the character and extent of output, but specifying the terms of service and the amount of the wages payable in respect of all the workers in a particular factory, shop, or yard.

Under a contract of this kind the Trade Union guarantees the output which has been agreed upon, arranges the necessary supervision of the workers, controls the engagements and dismissals of the foremen, and receives from the employer a lump sum in respect of wages, which is then distributed among the workers by the particular factory or workshop Committee concerned.

The policy of the Collective Contract has made little headway up to the present, but it is clear that, where the workers succeed in inducing an employer to agree to such a contract, either in a complete or in a modified form, they gain as a result valuable experience in control, while advancing a step in the direction of superseding the capitalist employer.[1]

5

Communism and Anarchism

Introductory.

A METHOD of treatment which includes Communism and Anarchism within the bounds of the same chapter demands some justification. Communists claim to be the inheritors of the true teaching of Karl Marx; yet the Anarchists under Bakunin joined issue with the followers of Marx on important points of doctrine. At the fourth Congress of the First International held at Bâle in 1869 these differences came to a head, and in 1872 Bakunin and the Anarchists were expelled from the

[1] The formation in 1919 of a Building Guild controlled by representatives from the local Management Committees of the various Building Trade Unions constitutes the first concrete experiment on Guild Socialist lines that has been undertaken. The subsequent failure of the Guild must be attributed to the difficulty necessarily experienced by an avowedly Socialist experiment which endeavours to introduce itself into a capitalist society, rather than to any defects inherent in the Guild idea.

Marxist International. The controversy between the two bodies centred chiefly round the question of the functions of the State. The German and English followers of Marx believed, at any rate at that time, in the retention of the State in some form after the Socialist revolution had been consummated; while the Italians and French repudiated the State altogether, chiefly on the ground of a total disbelief in the machinery of representative Government. The rejected Anarchists subsequently formed a Federal Union, which broke entirely with the Marxist Council of the International.

Despite these early differences, however, modern developments have tended to bring the two schools of thought into close relationship. Communism under the influence of the Russian Bolsheviks has become almost exclusively a philosophy of method—a theory, that is to say, of the manner in which the transition from Capitalism to Socialism is to be effected; Anarchism enunciates the principles which will operate in society after the transition has been effected. While Anarchists are concerned with the kind of society which they desire to see established and the way of life which they wish men to lead,[1] Communists are occupied with the problem of how to bring about that kind of society and to realize that way of life; the latter, that is to say, are concerned with means, the former with ends. To put the matter in another way, most Communists would now subscribe to the Anarchist ideal of society, while many Anarchists would probably agree that the methods advocated by the Communists are those most calculated to realize their ideal. Prince Kropotkin, the most prominent Anarchist writer, is in fact known as the apostle of 'Anarchist Communism'; and it is precisely with his conception of the ultimate state of Socialist society, as opposed to its

[1] There existed, and still exists, in Russia a so-called Nihilist Anarchism concerned with means rather than with ends, but from the point of view of political theory its influence is not important.

intervening transitional stage, that modern Communist theory is most closely in accord.

In treating of Communism and Anarchism in the same chapter, therefore, we are bringing together the two halves of the same whole. In the first section, on Communism, we shall be describing the philosophy of method which seeks to realize the type of society which will form the subject of the second.

I. *Communism.*

Communism is a word with many different meanings. Sometimes it is used to denote a theory of society, such as that of the early Christians, in which all property is held in common; at other times it is used synonymously with Socialism; it is also the name given to a system under which food, clothing, medical care, and other necessaries are freely administered according to want. We shall be concerned in this chapter, however, only with the special meaning which is given to the word Communism in the *Communist Manifesto*, the work of Marx and Engels, published in 1847, since this is the only sense of the word which denotes a special political theory distinct from that of any other school of Socialism.

Communism in this sense of the word is essentially a theory of method; it seeks to lay down the principles upon which the transition from Capitalism to Socialism is to be accomplished; and its two essential doctrines are the class war and the revolutionary—that is, the forcible—transference of power to the proletariat.

A. *Marxian Communism.* The leading features of Marx's work have already been briefly glanced at in chapter 3. It will, however, be necessary both to recapitulate and to expand part of what has been said in order to formulate the principles upon which Communism is based.

Marx held that the era of Capitalism would come to an end

as the result of the contradictions inherent in the very nature of Capitalism. Of these contradictions the most important are, first, that Capitalism is compelled, in order that it may extract the surplus value on which it lives, to create and to concentrate a class-conscious proletariat in such a way as to make it organize for victory over the capitalism that created it; and second, that in an age of ever-increasing production the great mass of the people are without property, and that, so long as Capitalism persists, they must necessarily remain so. Since the proletariat have not sufficient buying power to purchase the goods which the industrial system produces in ever greater quantities, the capitalists are driven by the growing disparity between production and home consumption to seek new markets abroad, and to combine at the same time in ever larger trusts, which, in process of time, eliminate the small capitalist, and secure a monopoly of the class of goods concerned. As production increases, the competition for overseas markets grows fiercer; there is a rush to exploit and appropriate undeveloped territories, and Capitalism, passing through the stages of Imperialism and world war, reaches its climax.

The events of recent years are acclaimed by modern Communists as providing a remarkable illustration of the accuracy of Marx's predictions. Their interpretation of recent events is on the following lines. The origin of the world war was economic. The forces of production outstripped the existing social organization, with the result that goods were produced at such a rate that society could not control the use of them. Hence arose in a world of propertyless workers the vulgar display and ostentation of the idle rich together with an increasing competition for fresh markets, which, under the guise of Imperialism, produced war as the inevitable result. Lenin, for example, defines Imperialism as 'Capitalism in that stage of development in which monopolies and financial capital have attained a preponderating influence, the export of capital has acquired great importance, the international trusts have begun the partition of the world, and the biggest capitalist countries have completed the division of the entire territorial globe among themselves'. At this stage the contradictions in Capitalism lead to its overthrow. The proletarian class created by Capitalism is the force which destroys that which created it. Growing ever in numbers and in the insistence of its demands, it refuses ultimately to be satisfied with anything less than the expropriation of the exploiters, the social ownership of property which has hitherto been held privately, and the transference of power to the militant workers.

This uprising of the proletariat is not without previous parallels in history. In fact every class which has, at some time or another, been dominant in society, has been supplanted and suppressed by a class which the circumstances of its own dominance have brought into existence. Thus the *bourgeoisie*, created by feudalism, caused the overthrow of feudalism by means of the expansion of industry and the spread of commerce. But though history affords parallels to the uprising of the proletariat, the latter is in one respect unique. All previous revolutions have resulted in the suppression of a class by a class, in the usurpation of the power of a minority by a minority. But the victory of the working class carries with it the emancipation of humanity. Though the revolution itself is carried out on a class basis, the state of society which follows the revolution will be based on the abolition of classes. Thus the Communists hold that the battle they are fighting, though outwardly waged on behalf of a dispossessed class, is really the battle of the whole of mankind; and it is this conviction, embraced with the intensity born of a disinterested ideal, which generates the power of self-sacrifice and self-devotion underlying a superficially somewhat arid and doctrinaire programme.

But though the emancipation of humanity and the abolition of classes is the Communist's ultimate aim, it is one which cannot, in his view, be realized for many years. The revolution of the proletariat may pave the way to such a Utopia, but it does not miraculously bring it into being. We are thus led to the conception of two distinct stages of revolutionary progress, a conception anticipated by Marx and adopted by the Communists: (1) a transitional, revolutionary stage based on the domination of the State by the working class; (2) a communistic, classless stage, in which the State as a repository of authority has vanished. It will be convenient to consider each of these two stages separately.

(1) *The Revolutionary Stage.* The Communists chiefly dissent from the doctrines of the evolutionary Socialists described in chapter 3 in holding strongly that no fundamental change can be made in the structure of society without important modifications in the State. The experience of the past, and especially of the Paris Commune of 1871, has taught them that the working classes cannot simply take over the machinery of the existing capitalist State and use it for their own purposes. The existing State machine is essentially unsuited for revolutionary purposes; its officials are unreliable, its procedure ineffective, and its nature incapable of being changed by a mere change of masters. The conquest of political power by a workers' party is, accordingly, of little or no value so long as the capitalist remains in possession of the instruments of production. In virtue of this possession the capitalists will always be able to ensure that a Parliament dominated by a constitutional Labour party will only pass legislation of a type which will leave their industrial power untouched. Even if such a party were to attempt to pass legislation expropriating the capitalists and transferring their property to the Community, they would evade its regulations, or, in the last resort, fight in defence of their privileges. It is held that the growth of the power of the Labour party in Great Britain, coupled with their comparative failure to make any impression upon the dominance of the Capitalists, fully bears out this view.

It is argued, accordingly, that constitutional means must be abandoned, the machinery of the existing State superseded, and a revolutionary dictatorship of the proletariat proclaimed. Modern Communists have never hesitated to emphasize the severity and bitterness of the struggle which will accompany the overthrow of the capitalist class. Armed violence will be necessary on the part of the workers, not only to dispossess the capitalists, but to resist counter-revolutions designed to restore them. As Engels says, ' The party which has triumphed in the revolution is necessarily compelled to maintain its rule by means of that fear with which its arms inspire the reactionaries. If the Commune of Paris had not based itself on the authority of the armed people against the *bourgeoisie*, would it have maintained itself more than twenty-four hours? '

In this connexion it is pointed out that the *bourgeoisie* have all the advantages of superior education, discipline, and military talent. They have fighting materials at their disposal and money for their equipment. It is not to be expected, therefore, that even if dispossessed by a sudden revolutionary *coup*, they will refrain from using these advantages.

' In any and every serious revolution ', says Lenin, ' a long, obstinate, desperate resistance of the exploiters, who for many years will yet enjoy great advantages over the exploited, constitutes the rule. Never . . . will the exploiters submit to the decision of the exploited majority without making use of their advantages in a last desperate battle or in a series of battles.' Thus ' the transition from Capitalism to Communism forms a whole historical epoch '.

During this epoch what Lenin calls a ' quasi-State ' of the workers will be created in place of the existing bourgeois State. This new State will of necessity be a class organization, but it will function as the representative of the revolutionary working class. ' In order to break down the resistance of the *bourgeoisie* ', says Marx, 'the workers invest the State with a revolutionary and temporary form.' It follows that the State during this period will be oppressive and autocratic; it will exercise compulsory powers, and it will not be purely democratic; that is to say, it will not represent all the parties within the State. On the contrary, it will represent one party only, the proletariat, and will be definitely used by that party to suppress the *bourgeoisie*.

'Since the State', says Engels, 'is only a temporary institution which is to be made use of in the revolution in order forcibly to suppress the opponents, it is perfectly absurd to talk about a free, popular State: so long as the proletariat needs the State, it needs it not in the interests of freedom, but in order to suppress its opponents; and when it becomes possible to speak of freedom, the State as such ceases to exist.'

These quotations have been given because the extent to which the Communist movement is or is not a democratic movement is a much debated question (to which we shall return later). It is sufficient to point out here that, so far as the transitional revolutionary period is concerned, democracy in the ordinarily accepted sense of the word is regarded as being neither practicable nor desirable.

(2) *The Post-Revolutionary Stage.* In suppressing the *bourgeoisie* the State is encompassing its own downfall; for in so far as it is successful in this aim it becomes superfluous. Being an organization formed on a class basis to advance class interests, it ceases to have any *raison d'être* so soon as it has suppressed class distinctions. It will then, in Lenin's words, 'wither away', giving place to a free society of voluntary associations formed for the transaction of public business. It is this society, whose advent bears witness to the fact that the revolutionary era has terminated, which is in effect the state of complete freedom for which Anarchism works, and we shall describe it more fully in the second half of this chapter.

B. *Recent developments in Communist theory.* The above constitutes a brief account of those aspects of Marx's doctrine which have been emphasized and developed by modern Communists. That Marx's writings are susceptible of a different interpretation, upon which a wholly different philosophy of method can be based, we have already seen in tracing the growth of evolutionary or Collectivist Socialism in chapter 3. Recent events, and in particular the Russian Revolution of 1917, besides giving to Communism an immense practical importance, have not unnaturally led to fresh developments on its theoretical side. These developments take the form not of a recantation of Marx's teaching, but rather of an added emphasis which has been placed upon certain aspects of it at the expense of others. Russian Communism has given, as it were, a peculiar twist to Marx's work without in any way abandoning its substance. As a result of this twist Communists have recently been led to bestow much more attention than they have hitherto done upon the question of 'democracy', and much of Lenin's writing, and in particular his celebrated reply to Kautsky,[1] is devoted to the question of how far and in what sense Communism is democratic.

In order to understand how this question came to receive its present importance, we must retrace our steps and glance briefly at the history of the Communist movement during the last half-century. The Second International, formed in 1889, was in basis purely Marxist, but it was one of the least militant bodies that have ever professed Marx's principles. It is true that its constitution implied a much higher degree of organization among the workers than had existed at the time of the First International, the last thirty years of the nineteenth century and the first decade

[1] Kautsky published at Vienna in 1919 a pamphlet called *The Dictatorship of the Proletariat*, which contained a violent criticism of Communist principles and methods as practised in Russia, mainly on the ground that they involved a departure from the true doctrine of Marx.

of the twentieth having witnessed a great growth both in the strength and in the numbers of the workers' organizations.

But with increase of organization came a decrease in revolutionary spirit. The age was a peaceful one, an age of great industrial expansion, an age of comparative plenty. Concessions were consequently obtained from the possessing classes with an ease which seemed to convict Marx's prophesies of undue pessimism, and hopes were entertained that the transition to Socialism would be accomplished, gradually indeed, but peacefully, through the exercise of working class strength at the polls. But these hopes were illusory.

Even before the world war there had been the Syndicalist revolt based on a more militant interpretation of Marx's principles, and the world war brought revolutionary, international Socialism into the field again as an active and growing force. The war helped the militants in many ways; but it helped them most of all by driving so effectual a wedge between the revolutionary and the evolutionary Socialists that it is doubtful whether the two wings of Socialism will ever again form part of the same movement. The war forced men to choose between allegiance to class and loyalty to nation, and, the choice once made, events rendered it increasingly difficult for them to go back on their decision.

Those who were swayed by national loyalty were brought into the closest possible touch with the national Governments which their Socialist creed required them to distrust, and gave themselves to the task of exhorting the workers to enlist for the purpose of killing other workers whom the International taught them to regard as their brothers. Some Socialists even held office in bourgeois Governments.

Those who took the other line found themselves driven by the pressure of events equally far in the contrary direction. Persecuted and imprisoned by the various belligerent States for their refusal to defend nations which were in each case represented as the victims of unpardonable aggression, their attitude developed into an implicit denial of the whole State conception. In war time a citizen can logically refuse to defend the State to which he happens to belong only by disowning its authority, or, at any rate, by putting before it the authority of some other body, and this was in fact the line which the revolutionary Socialists took. Seeing in the world war a fulfilment of Marx's predictions, they proclaimed loyalty to the militant working class movement, disowned national divisions, and rallied to the Third International. This International was formed at Moscow in 1919 by the victorious Marxists, who had seized power in Russia in the 1917 Revolution. One of its most important acts was to draw up and publish an elaborate Manifesto which restates the principles of revolutionary Communism. In all essentials these are the same as those enunciated by Marx and Engels, which we have already described. A new feature, however, is the emphasis which is now laid on the necessary differences between militant Communism and the ordinary conception of democracy.

Communism and Democracy. In discussing this question the sharp distinctions which are drawn between capitalist society, the transitional revolutionary State, and the order of society which will one day succeed it, must be carefully borne in mind. As regards capitalist society, the Communist's attitude is based not so much upon a distrust of democracy as such, or upon a dislike of majority rule, as upon the conviction that, under existing conditions, democracy is not and cannot be a reality. So long as the mass of men are propertyless, it is idle to talk about individual freedom or about men's power of determining the order of society in which they live. There is no freedom for the individual, since, as he has no alternative but to sell his labour to the highest bidder, he can exercise no effective control with regard to the kind of life he wishes to lead. As regards the structure of Government, however democratic this may be in form, the repository of authority in society will be, not the Government, but those who possess economic power in virtue of their possession of the means of industrial production.

The fact that the workers are now given an apology for education, so far from putting them on an equality with their exploiters, only makes matters worse; the existence of a semi-educated proletariat enables the exploiters to rivet their chains more strongly. Controlling, as they do, education, the press, and the pulpit, they use these organs to 'dope' the minds of the workers, now rendered more easily accessible to capitalist influences. It is idle, therefore, to hope to win the whole mass of the workers, while all the instruments of propaganda are controlled by the other side. This state of affairs will continue until a situation arises, comparable to that produced by the war in Russia, when the class-conscious minority feel that they can act with some assurance of the support of the majority. It is to such a situation that Communists look to terminate the era of Capitalism, and they hold that it is futile in the meantime to expect a bourgeois democracy, that is to say a democracy deliberately impregnated with the views which are convenient to the bourgeois class, to will the suppression of that class.

As regards the transitional stage of the dictatorship of the proletariat, the case is somewhat different. Such a stage will be democratic in the sense that it can only continue for so long as the mass of the workers wills its continuance; but it will not be a pure democracy in the sense of commanding the assent of the people as a whole. A democracy of the exploited can no more express the real will of the exploiters than the existing democracy of the exploiters expresses the real will of the exploited.

Thus, before the revolutionary period pure democracy is found to be inoperative, and during the revolutionary period it is declared to be impracticable. It is upon the militant resolution and energy of will of the few, rather than upon the possibility of obtaining universal consent, that the Communists rely in the struggle against Capitalism. To many this may seem a gloomy and pessimistic outlook, and it is certainly the case that Communists differ from most other Socialists in believing that the struggle with Capitalism is inevitable, and will be both violent and protracted. They refuse, however, to admit that theirs is necessarily a policy of despair. They hold, on the contrary, that revolutionary Socialism is the only source of hope in an otherwise bankrupt world. Unless Capitalism is destroyed, its struggles will rapidly shatter civilization. War will succeed war, pestilence will succeed famine, until society goes down beneath the destructiveness of the forces of unchecked Capitalism. Each fresh war destroys all the petty gains that the forces of peaceful Socialism and Liberalism have won; they are swept aside in moments of danger, and reaction naked and unashamed takes their place. If, then, the world is to be saved from the evils of a capitalist civilization which has outlived its function in the evolution of society, salvation can only come from a strong and resolute revolutionary party, with the determination to overthrow Capitalism when the moment comes, and the knowledge of how to replace it.

II. *Anarchism.*

Lenin held the view, and it is a view with which most Communists would agree, that, after the dictatorship of the proletariat has served its purpose, the machinery of the State will be destroyed.

The 'quasi'-State based on the power of the workers will in its turn 'wither away' and give place to what is called a 'free organization' of society. It is this 'free organization' of society which Anarchism advocates. It is described by Kropotkin, its chief literary exponent, as 'a principle or theory of life and conduct under which society is conceived without government—

PRINCE KROPOTKIN

G 2

harmony in such a society being obtained not by submission to law, or by obedience to any authority, but by free agreements concluded between the various groups, territorial and professional, freely constituted for the sake of production and consumption, as also for the satisfaction of the infinite variety of needs and aspirations of a civilized being'.

With regard to the question of how such a state of society is to be brought about, Anarchism has little to say. Kropotkin does indeed claim that the Anarchist conception of society, far from being an impracticable Utopia, is derived from an analysis of the tendencies existing and growing in the community to-day. He supports this claim by pointing to the enormous simplification in the provision of the necessaries of life which the growth of machinery has rendered possible, and to the great increase in voluntary associations formed for other than political purposes. But although the facts to which he refers are undoubted, it is questionable whether they do tend altogether in the direction he supposes; it is doubtful, that is to say, whether in the natural course of evolution society will, short of a revolutionary upheaval, develop altogether on Anarchist lines. The most that can be affirmed with certainty is the existence of the marked tendency in the direction of anti-authoritarianism and devolution of functions described in the second chapter. This tendency is in accordance with the 'localism' which is so prominent a feature of Anarchism, and it is in direct opposition to the disposition to centralize which is characteristic of Marxian Communism.

In the present chapter we shall confine ourselves to a consideration of Anarchism as an ideal, and we shall not ask how it is to be realized, since to this question Communism supplies the answer with which most Anarchists would agree.

Anarchists claim that only in an Anarchist society would the individual be able to develop his full nature and to realize all that he has it in him to be. This complete development of individuality would be rendered possible by the entire absence of external restraints: the individual would in fact for the first time be really *free*. If we ask what he would be free from, the answer is, 'From every kind of authority,' and by enumerating the various kinds of authority from which Anarchism seeks to free the individual, and the reasons which it gives for wishing to do so, we shall most readily obtain an insight into its character.

The sources of authority from which Anarchism would emancipate the individual may be reduced to three:

(1) It would free man as a producer from the yoke of the capitalist.

(2) It would free man as a citizen from the yoke of the State.

(3) It would free man as an individual from the authority of religious morality derived from hypothetical, metaphysical entities, such as an omnipotent God.

This third aspect of Anarchism raises ethical questions which fall outside the scope of the present book, while the first, consisting of an indictment of Capitalism on economic and moral grounds, is familiar, and need not be restated. We shall content ourselves, therefore, with a description of the second, which is in a very real sense peculiar to Anarchism.

Is Government necessary? On the economic side Anarchism expresses itself in the belief in a universal Communism which is stated by Kropotkin as follows: 'All belongs to every one. And provided each man and woman contributes his or her share for the production of necessary objects, they have a right to share in all that is produced by everybody.'

The question immediately arises, 'Is not some form of Government necessary to ensure that everybody's share is just?' The Anarchist answer, as opposed to that of the Marxian Communist, is emphatically in the negative. He urges on the contrary that the chief function of Governments hitherto has been to ensure that everybody's share is unjust.

So far as autocracies and oligarchies are concerned the truth of this proposition is obvious. The rule of the one or of the few is clearly incompatible with equal power on the part of every one, and, if it is not in theory incompatible with equal possessions, it has always been employed to ensure a disproportionate share of the world's goods to those who possessed the power.

But is the proposition true as regards representative Government based on majority rule? The Anarchist contends that it is. He further contends that not only the State as it exists to-day, but any form of State that could or might exist in the future is both unnecessary and injurious.

The following are the main reasons for his contentions:

A. *Distrust of the existing State.* The State as it exists to-day is used by the few as an instrument to protect their unjust monopolies of those things which rightly belong to all. For this very reason, therefore, the State cannot be used to accomplish the abolition of the monopolies it protects. It follows that, until the State is replaced by some organization other than the State, Capitalism and private property can never pass away. The State, in short, can never be seized and used, as some Socialists suggest, for the purpose of inaugurating a new era of society.

For this reason Anarchists are opposed to any extension of the present functions of Government, even when they appear to be in the interests of the masses, nor do they encourage working men to join political parties or to obtain election to national Parliaments.

B. *The fallacy of Representative Government.* The above arguments are valid not only against existing States but against any possible reconstruction of the State. For it is the nature of the State to be a nationally representative body which exercises authority. Now the State cannot seek the will of the people on any and every question as it arises, and must, therefore, if it is not to be an open tyranny, be carried on by means of representative

Government. Hence the theory of representative democracy envisages the election by the people at large of a number of persons who will represent and carry out their wishes for a given term of years. But no man can adequately represent another man, much less a body of other men. In the first place he has not the knowledge necessary to enable him to deal adequately with all the questions that arise for decision. A man knows and can know nothing but what he practises, and in every department of affairs those are best fitted to direct who are themselves the workers in that department. Representative Government is, therefore, government by men who know just enough about everything to enable them to do everything badly, and not enough about anything to enable them to do anything well. It generates the professional politician (professional, that is, in the sense that it is his profession to substitute professions for knowledge), the professional lawyer, and the professional priest, general dealers in human relationships whose business it is to perpetuate the human weaknesses on which they are nourished. Thus politicians will draw boundaries without any proper knowledge of ethnology or geography, and lawyers decide questions of will, purpose, and motive with the crudest knowledge of psychology. Anarchism, therefore, evinces itself rather surprisingly as a plea for direction by experts rather than for government by amateurs.

In the second place the Common Will expresses itself differently with regard to each one of the questions that the State has to settle. Either the representative has to work in the dark, which is not to the advantage of those he represents, or he will have to call a meeting of his constituents every time a question arises for settlement, and get them after discussion to formulate an expression of their will. But in this latter event his office will be unnecessary.

With regard to the representative system, then, it may be said either that it is unnecessary or that it does not represent. The only method of securing real representation of the Common Will is to convene a meeting of the people affected, to appoint an *ad hoc* delegate to express the will of the meeting with regard to the particular question which they have discussed, and to cease to consider him a representative so soon as he has conveyed and expressed the will of the people on the matter in question. In no circumstances should the delegate be allowed to make laws dealing with matters other than that in respect of which he has been chosen as delegate.

The method proposed amounts to a repudiation of the belief in the efficiency of representative Government, and is accordingly considered shocking by the average democrat; yet it is the method to which learned societies and business men always resort when they wish to come to an agreement and to express their agreement on any particular point.

C. *Effect of Power.* The exercise of power over other men inevitably corrupts the best intentioned natures. It makes them selfish, arrogant, and oppressive, seekers after their own ends and neglectful of the interests of those who place them in power. The politician, for example, is wicked not because of his nature but because of his position; not because he is a man but because he is a politician. No man and no body of men should, therefore, be entrusted with governmental authority over their fellows.

In contradiction, therefore, to the charge that in proposing to dispense with Government based on force he is placing undue trust in his fellows, the Anarchist retorts that he is in fact unduly distrusting them. It is because the Anarchist distrusts human nature that he will not let it govern, preferring to say with Kropotkin, 'This or that despicable minister might have been an excellent man, if power had not been given to him'.

But the love of power which government fosters can only be nourished on the exercise of power, and the exercise of power necessarily requires persons over whom it may be exercised.

Therefore Governments from their very nature use force, force to separate men who are naturally friends into different and hostile nationalities, force to separate men who are naturally brothers into different and hostile classes. Thus the evils of internal strife and external war arise directly, in the Anarchist view, from the fact of Government; to quote the Anarchist speaker in Mr. Lowes Dickinson's *Modern Symposium*, 'Government means compulsion, exclusion, distraction, separation; while anarchy is freedom, union, and love. Government is based on egotism and fear, anarchy on fraternity. It is because we divide ourselves into nations that we endure the oppression of armaments; because we isolate ourselves as individuals that we invoke the protection of laws.'

D. *Why the State is superfluous.* The Anarchist supports his indictment of the State as superfluous by concrete illustrations. He asks, for example, 'Is the State necessary for education?' and answers that it is not. If the mass of the workers are only given enough leisure to instruct themselves, those among them who are fond of tuition will be only too eager to instruct the others, and numbers of voluntary educational societies will spring up anxious to outrival each other in excellence of teaching.

Is the State necessary for defence against foreign aggression? Again the answer is in the negative. Standing armies, says Kropotkin, are always beaten by invaders, who have historically been repulsed only by spontaneous uprisings unorganized by the State.

The record of the State in guaranteeing security to the individual is no better. So far from protecting the citizen from ill-disposed persons it creates them. It drives men to crime through the misery caused by its ill-adjusted economic system, and then punishes them for its own handiwork by throwing them into prison, thereby confirming their criminality for the future by making it impossible for them to earn a living by honest means.

In art, in science, and in business, the departments of human activity in which most energy is displayed and most progress achieved, the State does not presume to interfere, the free activities of men in these spheres being expressed in voluntary organizations, clubs, academies, and societies. The bodies which regulate these activities, such as the Royal Society and the British Association, rely for the transaction of necessary affairs not upon compulsion but upon free co-operation.

As for business matters, Kropotkin cites as an illustration of his thesis the arrangements made for the conduct of international railway traffic. A traveller from Madrid to Moscow travels along railroads constructed by millions of workers, in trains set in motion by dozens of companies. Yet the very complicated arrangements needed to ensure a smooth journey have been carried out as the result of the purely spontaneous efforts of the parties interested. Free co-operation is substituted for compulsion, and voluntary arrangement for enforced regulations.

Organization of a free society. It is in this direction then that we are to look for the structure of society that is to supersede the State. When we ask how order is to be maintained and public business to be transacted when the State is abolished, the answer is, by voluntary associations formed *ad hoc* for the carrying out of special purposes. Each trade and business should be conducted by a society voluntarily formed by all those who choose to engage in it, which will elect and remove its own officials, determine its own policy, and co-operate by free arrangements with other similar bodies. A complex interweaving of associations with order everywhere and compulsion nowhere, forms the stuff of which an Anarchist society will be made. For Anarchy, as Mr. Lowes Dickinson's speaker puts it, 'is not the absence of order; it is the absence of force'.

These associations, groups, and federations will be of all sorts of sizes and degrees, and they will be formed for all sorts of different purposes. Harmony will be achieved in society by the equilibrium of these forces and influences. The use of the word equilibrium should not be taken to suggest that an Anarchist society will be stagnant, a society of static perfection; on the contrary, the influences of the various free associations that form society will be continually changing in degree and direction, so that the equilibrium between them will require constant re-adjustment. But where there is no favoured association or privileged class, where, moreover, there is no State to protect one society at the expense of another, such equilibrium will be easier of attainment than it would be under existing conditions. Voluntary societies will exist for the fulfilment of every purpose that men have in common; some will be formed on a vocational basis, others on a territorial, and they will between them carry out the whole of the functions at present monopolized by the State. Thus, to adopt a modern terminology, Anarchism is first and foremost a plea for decentralization, both territorial and functional. It bases the structure of society on the smallest association whether of the village or of the workshop, and believes that the rest of the social organism will develop freely from this basic unit. The development will be always in the nature of a development from the more simple to the more complex, so that, instead of the simplest and smallest group being the least important, as in the society of to-day, it will, under Anarchism, become the most important, being in fact the peg from which the whole structure depends.

When we put the obvious question, 'Who then will see to the adjustment of interests, the prevention of friction, and the maintenance of goodwill between the various groups?' the answer is that when people are properly educated, when there is no inequality between rich and poor to provoke discontent, and no State protection of monopolists to inflame it, interests will rarely conflict, and occasions of disharmony will be few.

LENIN

People whose initiative is not sapped by Governmental grandmotherliness, and whose interests are not thwarted by Governmental interference, will develop freely, and with free and full development the sentiment of sociability will grow to a hitherto undreamed of extent. It is competition which breeds enmity; eliminate competition, therefore, and men's natural friendliness will grow and deepen until, instead of seeing in each alien group a rival to be feared, or an enemy to be overcome, they will regard it as a friendly society needing and inviting their welcome co-operation.

It is argued, then, that the operation of the principle of free arrangement and free combination will produce a natural grouping of society, and that the natural grouping, as compared with the artificial groupings which have so far been imposed upon men by Governments, will be so harmonious, so satisfying, and so efficient, that it will not easily be disturbed by quarrels and disputes, even if, which is unlikely, such were to arise.

'Take pebbles', says Fourier, 'put them into a box and shake them, and they will arrange themselves into a mosaic that you could never get by entrusting to any one the work of arranging them harmoniously.'

The above is a brief and necessarily vague outline of the Anarchist theory of society. It is necessarily vague because the theory, though simple in outline, exists in outline only. From its simplicity, which it shares in common with all extreme views, it derives much of its plausibility; but it is to be feared that this plausibility is delusive, arising in a large measure from the refusal or inability of the supporters of Anarchist theory to fill in the details of this attractive outline.

As to the wisdom of Anarchists in proposing to dispense altogether with the State, both as a central body and as the repository of force in the community, we shall offer some observations in the succeeding chapter.

6

Problems of Socialist Theory

THE various forms of Socialist doctrine described in the last three chapters raise a number of important questions. Many of these questions are highly controversial, and it is doubtful whether there is anything which can be asserted with regard to them which could not with an equal show of reason be denied. At the same time our survey would not be complete without a consideration of some of the issues involved, which are of particular practical importance at the present time.

Our consideration must necessarily be brief, and it will be confined to three important questions. These are (1) the psychological question whether Socialism provides men with a sufficient incentive to do the world's work; (2) the question of functional democracy; and (3) the merits of the different methods for bringing about a Socialist society advocated respectively by the evolutionary and the revolutionary Socialists.

(1) *The Incentive to work.* The question whether men could be induced to work except for their own pecuniary profit lies, as we have seen, at the root of all forms of Socialism, and unless the assumption which Socialists make with regard to it is justified, all forms of Socialism would fail in practice. The opponents of Socialism commonly urge that men will only work, or will only work well, for themselves, and that considerations of the social good leave the average man cold. It follows that the incentive of doing better than one's neighbour, and so of obtaining a greater share of the world's goods, is the only one of sufficient driving power to ensure that the existing level of production will be maintained. Hence the only possible basis for society is that of private profit and competition.

Upon the validity of these arguments it is not possible in the present state of our experience to pronounce with any certainty.

The following considerations may, however, be advanced to show that they are at any rate not conclusive.

(*a*) The assumption underlying the anti-Socialist position seems to be that men naturally dislike work. This assumption is highly dubious. It is true that men nourish an unreasoning prejudice against work at present, but that is because they suffer so frequently from dull work and overwork. A man who spends eight or nine hours a day in the monotonous repetition of some trivial manual process naturally imagines Utopia as a place in which he would do nothing at all, his enthusiasm for Utopian idleness being quickened by the knowledge that the chief purpose of his present labour is to make money for somebody else. Most men spend two-thirds of their working lives in obtaining the means to make life possible, and only one-third in enjoying the residue of life that remains. In these circumstances they are led to suppose that where the means of life are supplied gratis, the sum of human aspirations would be sufficiently satisfied by the enjoyment of them. But this supposition is erroneous. Most men like work, though they like it in moderation, and would discover a life of mere enjoyment to be a life of complete boredom. 'The best definition of hell', said Shaw, 'is a perpetual holiday'; and for most of us it is true that the best recipe for happiness is not to have leisure enough to wonder whether we are miserable.

The behaviour of the retired business man who, having made his pile, seeks to enjoy it, illustrates our thesis. Having worked all his life at making money, he finds himself so bored with unlimited leisure that he has to work at something else. He accordingly pays large sums for the privilege of working at some dangerous or laborious hobby, such as mountain climbing, desert exploring, or yacht racing, in which other people can only be induced to accompany him on the payment of a considerable salary. Failing this, he usually ends by returning to business and continuing to make money which he does not want, in despair of making life tolerable without the hard labour to which he has been accustomed.

Some men, tramps and artists for instance, naturally dislike work; but the temperament of the tramp who will do nothing, or of the artist who will only do the work he really wants to do, is rare. Effort is natural to men, and, if they cannot work for themselves, they will insist on working for somebody else.

As Kropotkin puts it: it is 'Overwork that is repulsive to human nature, not work. . . . Work, labour, is a physiological necessity, a necessity of spending accumulated bodily energy, a necessity which is health and life itself.'

What is required, then, is to make work more varied in quality and less burdensome in quantity. If this were done, there is a reasonable prospect that most men would cheerfully perform it.

But what about the dirty work, the dull work, and the dangerous work? Would men willingly do that except to enrich themselves? The answer to this question leads us to our second consideration.

(*b*) It would be possible in a community based on the principle of social service and not on that of private profit enormously to diminish the amount of dirty and unpleasant work. This diminution could be effected by the application of scientific knowledge to industry. Science is applied to industry at present, but it is only applied when it pays. It frequently does not pay to employ machines to do dirty, unskilled work, because unskilled labour can be obtained more cheaply. Thus men are still employed in appallingly unhygienic conditions in the stokeholds of steamers to stoke the furnaces, simply because the installation of stoking machinery would diminish the profits of the Company. To quote Kropotkin again: 'If there is still work which is disagreeable in itself, it is only because our scientific men have never cared to consider the means of rendering it less so; they have always known that there were plenty of starving men who would do it for a few pence a day.' If industry were run for the benefit of the community as a whole, and due regard paid to the comfort of the workers in the industry as being themselves members of the community, all the resources of science would be devoted to the object of eliminating dirty or unpleasant work, or contriving mechanical means for its performance. The performance of any such work that might still remain could be ensured by offering special inducements, either in terms of cash or social credit, to persons willing to perform it.

(c) *The Motive of Social Service.* It is commonly held that the motive of social service leaves men cold. This belief is a delusion. It is by appealing to the motive of social service, or as the cynic would have it, to the desire to obtain the credit and reputation that come to those who benefit their fellows, that society secures the performance of its most difficult and dangerous jobs. The volunteer who responds to the appeal to lead the forlorn hope is not moved to risk his life by the prospect of extra pay, but by a mixture of motives in which the purely heroic impulse is coupled with the desire to save his comrades, with, perhaps, a vision of the Victoria Cross pendant in the background.

Nor are these motives to be set aside as those of the exceptional man at the exceptional moment. In all small communities the desire to serve, to work for and to stand well with the community, is constantly operative, and is one of the most powerful factors in men's lives. The public schoolboy playing for his house, the monk scheming and daring for his religious order, are each giving expression to this desire. But the desire is not a piece of automatic mechanism always to be relied upon; to operate effectively it must be encouraged and kept alive by social recognition. At present it does not receive this encouragement. The chief organs of propaganda through which men's minds are reached, are owned and controlled by those whose interests are bound up with the continuance of the present system of competition. The virtues of business push and acumen, or in other words, of the capacity to go one better than one's neighbour and benefit oneself at his expense, are accordingly extolled, and the contrary social virtues of co-operation and subordination of self to the interests of the whole, are, except in war time, when the capitalist system is threatened from without and stands in need of them, ignored or even slighted.

What is true of the influences which reach the adult mind is even more true of those that form the youthful one. Education has much to say of patriotism, whereby the individual benefits the country to which he happens to belong by eliminating the citizens of other countries, but little enough of social service whereby the individual confers benefit by the elimination of his own profits. He is taught to fight for his country, but to work for himself. As a consequence the adolescent mind is unconsciously imbued with the belief that the only object of work is to obtain money for oneself and one's family, and that work for the community is Quixotic imbecility.

But a change in the scale of values which determine public opinion is not beyond the bounds of possibility. Public opinion is chiefly formed by two agencies, education and the press. By a change in the spirit of education and in the influences that control the press it would be possible to turn the current of opinion in the direction of valuing social effort as opposed to individual self-assertiveness. Practical effect could be given to such a change by bestowing the highest dignities and the richest rewards which the State had to offer, not upon those who had enriched themselves at the expense of the community, but upon those who, without seeking to advance themselves, had contributed most to the happiness or advancement of others.

It must be admitted, however, that the motive of social service, which Socialists hope would be developed by these means, would operate effectively only in small communities; and this consideration raises a question to which we shall return under the heading of Functional Democracy.

(*d*) *Payment for work under Socialism.* The argument that under Socialism idleness would prevail and production diminish becomes irrelevant when it is remembered that most forms of Socialism insist on a certain quota of work from each individual. The theory of the Collectivist Socialists is that, in general, work alone gives the right to the enjoyment of the produce of work, and one of their most serious charges against the present system is that many people enjoy wealth which has been produced by the labour of others. 'To consume without producing' is regarded by Collectivists as the greatest social sin, and it is unlikely, therefore, that, with certain exceptions in favour of the very old and the infirm, Socialists would be disposed to extend the necessaries of life to those who remained wilfully idle when there was work to do. There is no reason to suppose that the Guilds of producers envisaged under the Guild Socialist system would take a different view, and, so far as Communism is concerned, the conscription of labour in Russia has been harshly criticized as tyrannical by Western European writers. It is only Anarchism that proposes to distribute the common commodities to all applicants, without imposing any obligation to work. Anarchists assume that, in a society such as they advocate, practically every one would work. For the reasons given in (*a*) above, it is quite possible that this would be the case, and it might become increasingly the case the longer a Socialist *régime* lasted, and the more the prejudice against work, born of the competitive industrial system, faded away.

It would be rash, however, to assume that the Anarchist conception would be workable, at any rate for a very long time, and the Collectivist Socialist plan of insisting on the performance of some work by every citizen is more practicable. Such a plan necessarily involves the existence in the community of a body able in the last resort to draw upon a reserve of force, and Anarchism, which rejects the State, might accordingly find itself in a real difficulty over the question of work.

The objections to the Collectivist plan are those which apply to any form of compulsion. Work, it is said, must be performed before the individual is entitled to the necessaries of life. But who is to determine what kind of work is to count? Are painting pictures for which the world is not ready, or writing articles hostile to the Government, to be authorized as work?

The safest way is to leave such questions to be settled not by some central or local administrative body, but by the Guild of producers in which every citizen, whatever his calling, would, in a Guild Socialist State, be organized. The principle of functional democracy insists that questions of work and pay should be settled by functional bodies, and it is this principle which we must now briefly examine.

(2) *Functional Democracy.* Running like a strand through all the diverse theories we have been considering is the insistence on the importance of devolution. Syndicalists, Guild Socialists, and Anarchists, however much they may differ on other questions, are at one in this. The old conception of Socialism as a doctrine which would substitute unlimited State regulations for existing private arrangements, is no longer true. Even the Collectivists no longer maintain the doctrine of the omnipresent and all-pervasive State, with its army of skilled Civil Servants and ubiquitous inspectors—if indeed they ever did maintain it in anything like the extreme form attributed to them—so that, although the Guild Socialists parted company from them on this very issue, it is probable that they would now go in practice almost as far as the Guild Socialists themselves in their recognition of the importance of devolution, and of the exercise of control by local and functional, as opposed to national and central, bodies.

There exists to-day a general antipathy to centralized Government with its corollary of elaborate bureaucratic administration, to which we have already had occasion to refer in our first chapter on the philosophical theory of the State. Men, as we had occasion to note, belong to an increasing number of voluntary associations formed for different purposes, which cut right across the boundaries of the nation State, and are gradually usurping an increasing number of its functions as they have already usurped the great bulk of the interests of its citizens. It is no doubt to the growth of associations of this kind that Kropotkin refers when he speaks of the Anarchist conception of society as being derived from an analysis of tendencies existing in society to-day. While the significance of these associations for political theory remains in some respects obscure, this much, at least, seems clear, that the freshness and vitality of human association, and its capacity for stimulating the individual to the fullest development of his personality, have passed away from the State, in which they have resided in the past, and have become the attributes of other bodies smaller in size and various in character.

What the Greeks meant when they said, and said truly of the Greek City State, that it was only in society that a man could realize all that he had it in him to be, has ceased to be true of the political society we now call the State, and has become true of bodies representing a more limited range of interests, but representing them more directly.

It is to bodies of this kind, and not to the State, that Socialists increasingly look to evoke the enthusiasm for social service on which the practical effectiveness of Socialism necessarily depends. The reason for this change of outlook on the part of Socialists is to be sought mainly in the fact that the State has grown too big, too big, that is to say, to represent or express the wills of the individuals who compose it. So vast are the forces at work in society, so complex and elaborate the structure of Government, and so intricate and difficult to disentangle the factors that determine events, that, so far from controlling them, men are unable even to understand them. In face of the complex organism of society the individual feels helpless and impotent. Neither as a factor in the mythical General Will, nor as a distinct individual will can he influence the course of events. What does in fact happen seems to be not so much the result of human will and effort as of the interplay of blind and uncontrolled forces, whose genesis escapes detection and whose object, if any, is shrouded in mystery. In these circumstances thoughtful men sink into political apathy, or, if they think of politics at all, are driven to the interpretation of phenomena with which Mr. Hardy's novels have made us familiar, to the notion of a blind unfeeling Fate which, indifferent to human weal and woe, thwarts men without malignity and helps them without design. Thus a doctrine of unconscious political determinism prevails. Men feel that they are powerless to change the world in which they live, that they do not count in society, that their wills and wishes have ceased to matter. It is to this feeling that much of the current distrust of Socialist experiments is due: this distrust springs from a fatalistic outlook which, doubting if it is possible to change the structure of society, is nevertheless convinced that any change would involve a risk which it is better not to take.

It follows that if men's faith in social action is to be revivified, the State must be cut up and its functions distributed. It must be made possible for the individual to belong to a variety of small bodies possessing executive powers, dealing both with production and with local administration, as a member of which he can once again feel that he counts politically, that his will matters, and that his work is really done for society. This is what the Anarchist means when he says that society must be organized as a hierarchy of voluntary bodies, beginning with the simple and working upwards to the complex.

It would seem, then, that the machinery of Government must

be reduced in scale: it must be made manageable by being made local, so that, in seeing the concrete results of their political labours before them, men can be brought to realize that where self-government is a fact, society is malleable to their wills because society is themselves. It may well be that a society so constituted would be able to draw upon a well-spring of social service both in the workshop and on the workshop committee, which has run dry in the large-scale, centralized State. As regards the question whether a society of this type would find it necessary to retain a form of central authority bearing some resemblance to the existing State, it seems probable, for the reasons given in chapter 3,[1] that the existence of such a body would be necessitated by the fact that men's activities affect other men with whom they are not brought into direct personal relation. Some central body appears to be required to regulate such activities, and for this reason it is unlikely that an Anarchist society would in practice achieve that harmony which it contemplates.

(3) *The question of method.* The question of method is a difficult one, and an adequate discussion of the issues involved is outside the scope of the present book. Impatience with existing conditions and despair at the slowness of improvement generates in many Socialists a petulance which leads them to think that only a complete break with existing society will further the objects they desire. Modern Communists, as we have seen, follow Marx in regarding this break as necessarily of a violent character and such as to give rise to a prolonged period of civil war, and the Syndicalist doctrine of the General Strike is based upon the same belief.

It may well be doubted, however, whether the methods advocated by the revolutionary Socialists for eliminating Capitalism would produce the effects anticipated. It is, of course, the case that if the Marxian theory of historical determinism is right,

[1] See pp. 46–48.

the revolution is bound to occur so soon as economic circumstances are ripe for its occurrence, and the question whether Communists are wise in endeavouring to ensure that what must be will be, is therefore beside the point. If, in short, it is true to say that ideas play little or no part in determining events, it is irrelevant to consider whether some ideas are better than others.

If, on the other hand, the question of revolution is one which will in the long run be determined by human will and effort, it is pertinent to consider whether it were better to avoid revolution or to seek it.

In favour of avoiding it the following considerations deserve attention.

(*a*) During a period of violent conflict society goes into the melting pot; what shape it will assume when it emerges it is difficult, if not impossible, to predict. It is, however, safe to assume that it will differ very materially from the expectations which the promoters of revolution have formed of it. In particular it is probable that a revolutionary class war will place in a position of power a group of individuals who will be of an entirely different type from those who worked for the revolution in the days of Capitalism. Socialists are wrong in supposing that the rulers of a post-revolutionary State will resemble the men who now advocate unpopular changes from sheer disinterestedness. They will be of the ambitious, executive type, eager for power and pre-eminence, and anxious above all things to retain their positions. Because of the existence of such men, and of their tendency to obtain power at times of national conflict and danger, it seems unlikely that a society such as the Anarchists desire, in which there are no rulers, and men are for the first time really free, will emerge from the class war. Revolution seems, then, to involve a risk which wise men will prefer not to take.

(*b*) Violent changes promote violent reactions. In Russia, where the revolution was guided throughout by the doctrine of

Marxian Communism, it appears that, though the revolutionary party still retain power, the main principles for which they stood have come in practice to be abandoned. State Capitalism and private landlordism, bourgeois property-owning and private trading are the chief features of the situation in Russia to-day; with the result that the structure of society now bears as little relation to the teaching of Marx as it did in the pre-revolutionary era. There is no dictatorship of the proletariat in the present, and no prospect of the 'withering away' of the State and the coming of a free society in the future.

In these circumstances there seem to be good grounds for believing that the policy of gradual reform advocated by evolutionary Socialists is likely to secure advances of a more permanent, albeit of a less startling, character than the methods of the revolution and of the class war.

BIBLIOGRAPHY

THE two following books provide a general survey of the ground covered by the foregoing pages. Students may, therefore, find it useful to read them, especially in connexion with the first two chapters, before consulting the more specialized works mentioned below.

Ernest Barker. *Political Thought in England. From Herbert Spencer to the Present Day.* (Williams & Norgate, 1915.)

Ivor Brown. *English Political Theory.* (Methuen, 1920.)

CHAPTER I

T. H. Green. *Lectures on the Principles of Political Obligation.* (Longmans, 1895.)

B. Bosanquet. *Philosophical Theory of the State.* (Third edition. Macmillan, 1920.)

J. H. Muirhead. *The Service of the State.* (John Murray, 1908.)

Are representative books on the Idealist Theory of the State.

L. T. Hobhouse. *The Metaphysical Theory of the State.* (Allen & Unwin, 1918.)

H. J. Laski. *Authority in the Modern State.* (Yale University Press, Milford, 1919.)

Are written from a more or less critical standpoint.

CHAPTER II

J. S. Mill. *Utilitarianism, Liberty, and Considerations on Representative Government.* (Everyman's Library, 1910.)

Herbert Spencer. *The Man versus the State.* (Williams & Norgate, 1884; Watts & Co., 1909.)

—— *Social Statics.* (First edition, 1851.) (Abridged. Williams & Norgate, 1892.)

Are classical statements of nineteenth-century Individualism.

The Individualism of the twentieth century expresses itself in books by many different writers, which in other respects are often widely divergent in outlook and character. The following may be read:

Graham Wallas. *The Great Society.* (Macmillan, 1914.)

—— *Human Nature in Politics.* (Constable & Co. Third edition, 1920.)

Hilaire Belloc. *The Servile State.* (T. N. Foulis, 1912.)

Norman Angell. *The Great Illusion.* (Heinemann, 1913.)

J. N. Figgis. *Churches in the Modern State.* (Longmans, 1913.)

R. M. MacIver. *Community : A Sociological Study.* (Macmillan. Second edition, 1920.)

Bertrand Russell. *Principles of Social Reconstruction.* (Allen & Unwin, 1916.)

CHAPTER III

The Literature of Socialism is enormous and it is impossible to do more than to give a reference to a few of the most important books on the subject. The two best historical books are :

T. Kirkup. *History of Socialism.* (New edition revised by E. R. Pease.) (A. & C. Black, 1913.)

Max Beer. *History of British Socialism*, 2 vols. (G. Bell, 1919–20.)

Karl Marx's *Capital* (English trans., 2 vols.: (1) Trans. by S. Moore and E. Aveling. Sonnenschein & Co., 1887; (2) Abridged Popular Edition, trans. by S. L. Trask. International Bookshops, London, 1921) is the foundation of most modern Socialism.

Fabian Essays in Socialism. (Fabian Society, 1889. New edition, with introduction by Sidney Webb, 1920.)

J. Bruce Glasier. *The Meaning of Socialism.* (National Labour Press, Manchester, 1919.)

J. Ramsay MacDonald. *Socialism : Critical and Constructive.* (Cassell's Social Economics Series, 1921.)

William Morris and E. Belfort Bax. *Socialism, Its Growth and Outcome.* (Swan Sonnenschein & Co. Third edition, 1908.)

All contain a statement of Socialist principles.

The pamphlet published in 1918 by the British Labour Party, *Labour and the New Social Order*, indicates the immediate programme of the moderate British Socialists, and *A Constitution for the Socialist Commonwealth of Great Britain*, by Sidney and Beatrice Webb (Longmans, 1920), sketches a Constitution proposed for a society desiring to organize itself on Socialist principles.

The most important of the numerous writings hostile to Socialism are :

W. H. Mallock. *A Critical Examination of Socialism.* (John Murray, 1908.)

Hartley Withers. *The Case for Capitalism.* (Eveleigh Nash Co., 1920.)

CHAPTERS IV, V, VI

Bertrand Russell's *Roads to Freedom* (Allen & Unwin, 1918) contains a good account of Syndicalism, Marxism, and Anarchism, and may be read with advantage in connexion with all the subjects touched on in Chapters IV, V, and VI.

Syndicalism.

Most of the books on Syndicalism proper are in French. The most important are:

E. Pataud et G. Pouget. *Comment nous ferons la Révolution.* (Paris, 1909.)

Paul Louis. *Le Syndicalisme contre l'État.* (Paris, 1910.)

Georges Sorel. *Réflexions sur la violence.* (Third edition, Paris, 1912.) (English translation by T. E. Hulme. Allen & Unwin, 1916.)

Books in English are:

J. A. Estey. *Revolutionary Syndicalism.* (P. S. King, 1913.)

L. Levine. *Syndicalism in France.* (New and revised edition. P. S. King, 1914.)

J. Graham Brooke. *American Syndicalism.* (Macmillan, 1913.)

J. W. Scott. *Syndicalism and Philosophical Realism.* (A. & C. Black, 1919.) (Deals more particularly with the philosophy of Syndicalism.)

Guild Socialism.

A. J. Penty. *The Restoration of the Gild System.* (Swan Sonnenschein & Co., 1906.)

S. G. Hobson. *National Guilds.* (Edited by A. R. Orage.) (G. Bell & Sons. Third edition, 1919.)

G. D. H. Cole. *Self-Government in Industry.* (G. Bell & Sons. Third edition, 1918.)

—— *Guild Socialism Restated.* (Leonard Parsons, 1920.)

—— *Social Theory.* (Methuen & Co. Second and revised edition, 1920.)

M. B. Reckitt and C. E. Bechhofer. *The Meaning of National Guilds.* (C. Palmer & Hayward. Second and revised edition, 1920.)

Various publications of the National Guilds' League (39 Cursitor Street, E.C. 4).

Books hostile to Guild Socialism are:

G. C. Field. *Guild Socialism.* (Wells Gardner, Darton & Co., 1920.)

Graham Wallas. *Our Social Heritage.* (Allen & Unwin, 1921.)

Communism.

The classic statement of Communism is contained in *The Communist Manifesto* by Marx and Engels (1848); English translation published by William Reeves, 1888.

Max Beer. *The Life and Teaching of Karl Marx.* (1918.) (Translation by C. Partington and H. J. Stenning. Social Studies Series, vol. ii. National Labour Press, Limited, 1921.)

N. Lenin. *The Proletarian Revolution.* (The British Socialist Party, 1920.)

R. W. Postgate. *The Bolshevik Theory.* (Grant Richards, 1920.)

E. and C. Paul. *Creative Revolution.* (Allen & Unwin, 1920.) (Reprint, Plebs League, 1921.)

Books hostile to Communism are :

Karl Kautsky. *The Dictatorship of the Proletariat.* (Trans. by H. J. Stenning. National Labour Press, 1918 ; second edition, 1920.)

Bertrand Russell. *The Practice and Theory of Bolshevism.* (Allen & Unwin, 1920.)

Anarchism.

The great bulk of Anarchist writings is contained in pamphlets and in articles, in papers and reviews, and the number of books on Anarchism, especially of those in English, is small. The following are the most important :

P. Kropotkin. Freedom Pamphlets, No. 4. *Anarchist Communism.* (New Fellowship Press, 1891.)

—— No. 10. *Anarchism : Its Philosophy and Ideal.* (Third issue, 1904.)

—— No. 11. *The State : Its Historic Rôle.* (1902.)

(Books.)

Fields, Factories, and Workshops. (Swan Sonnenschein & Co, 1901 ; Nelson & Sons, 1919.)

Charlotte Wilson. *Anarchism.* (Fabian Tracts, No. 4.)

L. N. Tolstoy's *The Kingdom of God is within you* (trans. by Constance Garnett, 2 vols. W. Heinemann, 1893, 1894) is a literary statement of Anarchist Principles.

A work written from the Collectivist standpoint which contains a reasoned criticism of Anarchism is :

Alfred Naquet's *L'Anarchie et le Collectivisme.* (Paris, 1904.)